Nancy Crampton

Paula Fox is the author of a previous memoir, *Borrowed Finery,* which was a finalist for the National Book Critics Circle Award and won the PEN/Martha Albrand Award, as well as six novels, including *Desperate Characters, The Widow's Children,* and *Poor George.* She is also a Newbery Award-winning children's book author. She lives in Brooklyn, New York.

ALSO BY PAULA FOX

"In her acclaimed memoir *Borrowed Finery* (2001), Fox wrote with quiet power about her traumatic childhood. Now she writes about huge political upheaval, and once again she brings it close with small, intimate details. . . . You read the simple words slowly, and they haunt you."

—*Booklist*

"The picture Fox paints of postwar Europe is both profoundly beautiful and sad, and her memoir is affecting, leaving one wishing she had stayed there longer."

—*Publishers Weekly*

"Resonant . . . With her signature concision and understatement, Fox, now in her eighties, reassesses her past and extracts indelible insights. . . . Fox's minimalist prose evokes for the reader something other than ourselves—and the effect is deeply moving."

—*Newsday*

"A travel diary written in hindsight, this slender, elegant memoir is both hypnotic and sharply lucid. . . . Fox's vision encompasses history and humanity, thereby taking in so much more than the self."

—*Bust* magazine

THE
COLDEST
WINTER

A STRINGER IN LIBERATED EUROPE

PAULA FOX

Picador

Henry Holt and Company

New York

www.picadorusa.com

Picador® is a U.S. registered trademark and is used by Henry Holt and Company under license from Pan Books Limited.

For information on Picador Reading Group Guides, as well as ordering, please contact Picador.
Phone: 646-307-5629
Fax: 212-253-9627
E-mail: readinggroupguides@picadorusa.com

Designed by Kelly S. Too

Some of the chapters in this memoir have appeared elsewhere in slightly different form: "New York, New York" in *Dissent;* "After the Snow" in *The Paris Review* and *Pequod;* "Smile" in *The Threepenny Review;* "Children of the Tatras" in *Clarion Books;* "Perlita" in *HRI Quarterly;* and "Paris" in *The Paris Review.*

Illustration credits: page 3: Bettmann/CORBIS; page 5: Hulton-Deutsch Collection/CORBIS; page 19: John Springer Collection: CORBIS; page 26: Bettmann/CORBIS; page 30: Marc Garanger/CORBIS; page 37: Bettmann/CORBIS; page 43: Peter Turnley/CORBIS; page 46: Bettmann/CORBIS; page 56: Annette Fournete/CORBIS; page 64: Bettmann/CORBIS; page 72: author's private collection; page 96: Hulton-Deutsch Collection/CORBIS; page 104: Hulton-Deutsch Collection/CORBIS; page 107: Underwood & Underwood/CORBIS; page 118: Alinari Archives/CORBIS; page 122: Bettmann/CORBIS; page 132: Hulton-Deutsch Collection/CORBIS.

Library of Congress Cataloging-in-Publication Data

Fox, Paula.
    The coldest winter : a stringer in liberated Europe / Paula Fox.
       p. cm.
   ISBN-13: 978-0-312-42624-8
   ISBN-10: 0-312-42624-0
   1. Fox, Paula—Homes and haunts—Europe. 2. Authors, American—20th Century—Biography. 3. Stringers (Journalists)—United States—Biography. 4. Stringers (Journalists)—Europe—Biography. 5. Americans—Europe—Biography. 6. Europe—History—1945–I. Title.

PS3556. 094Z465 2005
813'.54—dc22

                                    2005040254

First published in the United States by Henry Holt and Company

First Picador Edition: November 2006

10 9 8 7 6 5 4 3 2 1

For Martin, always, and
for my acquired granddaughter, Sarah Greenberg

"Europe!"

—HENRY JAMES

NEW YORK, NEW YORK

I was born in New York City, and I have lived in or around it for a good part of my life. Some neighborhoods, although altered nearly beyond my recognition, are charged for me with the emotions of long-past events—at least during those moments I pass through them.

For what seemed one hundred years, I paid rent to landlords for wildly differing lodgings in various sections of the city. I was always trying to find a way to get out of New York during that time, a time when I imagined that if I could only find the right place, the difficulties of life would vanish.

The first time I recall glimpsing New York as a whole was from the deck of a Hudson River Dayliner when I was four or five years old. But perhaps I found the view of Riverside Drive and its towers oppressive, for I remember I soon returned to a spot near a railing from which I could stare down at the heads of the musicians of a band, two decks below, sitting on camp chairs and playing "Hail Columbia" for the pleasure of the passengers. Seventeen years later, in 1946, a year after the end of the Second World War, I saw the city again—from the outside—as I stood on the deck of a partly reconverted Liberty Ship on which I was sailing to Europe. I didn't look at it for long that second time either. I was getting away at last!

By then I had come to know New York well, the way you know a city where you've had jobs—most of them pretty awful—that keep you more or less fed and out of the weather. No matter what my circumstances were, I always found the city hard to live in. But there were moments of vividness and promise, even of glamour. It is startling to recollect them. As Cesare Pavese wrote in his diary, *The Burning Brand,* "Real amazement comes from memory."

People, some of them now names on headstones, were walking around the city in the days of my youth, and you might run into them in all sorts of places. I met Duke Ellington on a flight of marble steps leading down from an exhibit by the painter Stuart Davis. I heard Huddie (Leadbelly) Ledbetter play his guitar and sing "The Midnight Special" at a party in Greenwich Village for a cause I've forgotten. In a jazz club on 52nd Street that was called, I think, Kelly's Stable, Billie Holiday turned from the bar as I was passing and asked me—"Darlin', would you mind?"—to pick up her fur coat, which had fallen from her shoulders to the floor behind her bar stool.

Later that same evening, the club doors were shut and I was

among the people who stayed inside, sitting around a table, listening to her sing far into the night. I was escorted to the Savoy Ballroom in Harlem by a boyfriend, where I watched dancers bend and circle and hurl their partners into the air and, miraculously, catch them, to the music of two bands led by Cootie Williams and Lucky Millinder and then was, myself, drawn into the dance, wondering when the floor would give way and then not caring whether it did or did not. From Charles Street, where I borrowed a one-room apartment for a while, I could walk a couple of blocks to a bar on Seventh Avenue and hear Art Tatum play the piano for the price of a glass of beer, one dime.

One evening I went to Lewisohn Stadium to hear Paul Robeson sing. Planes flew overhead, and searchlights played against the sky. Quite suddenly, Robeson walked out onto the stage in a navy blue suit. He was so splendid in appearance, his profound basso so exalted, that the audience itself, I among them, seemed to feel an answering exaltation.

I met him twice after that concert, once in San Francisco during the run of *Othello* and a second time in New York City a few weeks after I had returned from Europe.

Memory often seems to begin in the middle of some story. I had a friend who was a friend of Robeson's. Robeson was spending time with his son, Pauli, who had come to the city from his prep school, somewhere to the north. I recall the four of us in a taxi, but not where we had met before catching it. We were going to a nightclub, Café Society Uptown, to hear a French chanteuse, Lucienne Boyer. There was conversation but I don't recollect saying a word, though I must have done so for I

remember Robeson looking at me and speaking, smiling. I stole a quick glance at his hands. Someone had told me that when he played football at Rutgers, his own teammates had deliberately trodden on his hands during practice sessions.

The doorman of the club and the maître d'hôtel who hurried toward us through a shadowed foyer, both recognized Robeson, at whose request we were taken to a small room with a balcony that overlooked the café's main space. Lucienne Boyer was singing in French as we sat down. She stood in a shower of light in a gold dress. She sang a few songs in English; one of them was "The Man I Love." Robeson hummed along with her, filling our little room with his plangent voice, though it was inaudible to the people sitting below. He whispered to me suddenly to sing too. I quavered out a few lines but then fell silent, overwhelmed at the thought of singing with Paul Robeson—well, almost singing.

Afterward we all went to Grand Central, where Pauli was to take a train back to school. It must have been nearly midnight. In those days, railroad stations were often deserted at such an hour. As we walked down the broad staircase, our footsteps echoed throughout the vast reaches of the terminal, where not even a single late traveler could be seen, hurrying to the last train home. The four of us could have been alone.

Then, from every corner, silently flying toward us like swallows, came the baggage porters in their red hats, converging on Robeson and his son as they reached the bottom step. He stood among them for several moments, talking and listening, laughing at something that one of the redcaps said to him. That is where the memory ends: Robeson on a step, laughing, his head thrown back, his son standing next to him, one of the porters gesturing toward a platform entrance as though Pauli's train was about to leave and they must run now to catch it.

I see the past differently as I grow older, so in a sense the past changes. I once thought it was the high emotional tone of that evening—its drama—that made it so memorable for me. Now I wonder if I did not feel some immense consolatory quality in Robeson's presence that was perhaps reflected on the faces of the redcaps. I don't really know.

HOW I EARNED MY PASSAGE

We emerged one by one from a large round hole in the ground, each of us, waiters and waitresses, bearing trays of food and drink for the patrons of a Catskills resort. It was early summer, 1946. My left arm was swollen and sore from the tetanus and typhus shots administered by a doctor in anticipation of my passage across the Atlantic Ocean to Southampton, England.

To distract myself from the soreness in my upper arm, I sometimes imagined the tips I might find among used glasses, dessert plates, and spilling ashtrays on the stained tablecloths when lunch or dinner was over. Those who tipped me at the end of their stay, rather than each day, would press pocket-warmed dollar bills into my hand.

The underground kitchen where we worked was connected to the upper world by a short spiral stairway. It was a hard climb upward, turning in a circle while carrying a full tray; sometimes one of them was dropped to the floor below. China crashed and fragmented, liquids splattered, food fell in repugnant lumps, the metal trays and covers banged and clattered, leaving silence in the wake of these disasters soon broken by our murmurs and cries of sympathy for the waiter or waitress whose tray had fallen and who was staring down in dismay at the underworld.

The dining room was thirty yards or so across a lawn, and its glass doors provided another hazard when they were closed against inclement weather. Yet it was a relief to be aboveground, out of the tight kitchen quarters and away from the predictable outbursts of the three bad-tempered cooks.

The male customers I waited upon called me *dear* or *darling.* Their wives or girlfriends gave me hard looks if they glanced up at me at all. Younger guests ignored me, except to send me back underground for more bread and water. I worked at the resort for five summer weeks, sleeping nights on a cot in a staff dormitory that smelled of unwashed socks and raw pine boards.

When I went back to New York City, I sublet a room in a tenement on Morton Street from an American Indian who was returning to his reservation in Arizona for a two-week visit.

There was, unaccountably, a shower stall standing in the center of the room that resembled a shaky voting booth. When I turned the taps, a spray of tepid water dropped on and past me to the grainy floor. I kept beneath the cot mattress a small roll of money I'd saved from the resort tips and my wages. The amount was enough to pay for my passage to England and, I estimated, a month of living in London.

The only window was close to the cot and gave onto a rusty fire escape. Beyond it was a narrow, dark airshaft.

Early one morning I awoke to find a young man crouched on the metal bars, staring at me through the open window, which I had flung up the night before. When he saw I was awake and staring back at him, he asked me for a cigarette, saying in a slurred voice that he had run out. He was fair-haired and thin, and his eyes held a reddish feral glow. I had a nearly empty crumpled pack of Camels beside the cot. I eased one out so it wouldn't break in two and handed him the rest of the pack; he muttered *thanks* and climbed back up the fire escape until he was out of sight. A few days later, I learned from the old Italian landlady that he'd overdosed on a drug she didn't identify and had been taken to a nearby hospital in an ambulance.

Decades later, at a party given by the painter Wolf Kahn on a Martha's Vineyard farm he had rented for the summer, I saw the red-eyed man again, recalling his face at once perhaps because he had startled me so—and frightened me, too, although I had not at the time recognized that fear. It came to me now. Wolf told me later his name was Miles.

He didn't recall the circumstances, but he remembered me too. I reminded him of the cigarettes I'd given him as he crouched on the fire escape. He pressed nearly a whole pack into my hand as we stood there on the hummocky ground. Both of us were struck by the same impulse; we bent forward and embraced, then stepped back and stood silently for several moments until Emily, also a painter and Wolf's wife, came between us with a plate of fresh corn.

THE SHIP I SAILED ON TO ENGLAND HAD BEEN MINIMALLY converted from its wartime function as a troop carrier. I wasn't troubled by its discomforts; I had hardly noticed them. I was departing from what was for me a land of sorrow. But it turned out that when the ship sailed one morning from New York City, my past followed me like its wake. On deck were the substantial ghosts of all the people I had ever known.

The journey took six days. One hot night, I was uncomfortable in my berth and went up to the top deck to sleep. I found a large group of people on deck in their nightwear, each one equipped with a pillow and a light blanket as I was, laughing and talking beneath a sky spangled with stars, some leaning on their elbows or sitting up and clasping their knees. Among them were several young people going to Yugoslavia to work on the "youth railroad" only for the glory of it.

One of them whom I knew, Kurt, who was eighteen, told me that night, or boasted, about his mistress, age thirty, and how she had wept when he said goodbye to her. He was a skinny boy, fluent and good-looking, well on his way to becoming a seducer of women. I could hardly have guessed that night, sitting with him, both of us covered with our blankets—it was chilly on deck—and talking with momentary intimacy, that I would meet him again four decades later at an Italian Center for the Arts that also held monthly conferences.

We recognized each other but had different memories of what had happened. He confided to a member of the bankers' conference he was attending that I had tried to draw him into a shipboard affair. I was happy to see him and recalled how he had spoken of his older lover on the voyage. For the five days the conference lasted, he smiled remotely at me. Once I heard what he had presumed to recollect, I stopped smiling back. I didn't ask him how he had liked Yugoslavia and the railroad.

One morning, seagulls began to circle the ship. Several hours later we landed at Southampton. From there, most of us took the train to London.

LONDON

During the summer, spent mostly in London, I stayed for varying periods of time, a few weeks or a month, with three couples. My father had given me the names of Benn Levy and his wife, Constance Cummings. Benn was an old friend of his from their days as screenwriters in Hollywood. The other two couples, Nan and her husband, Ted, and a journalist named Claude and his wife, Pat, I met through Maggie, a casual acquaintance of mine who, it was rumored, was an agent for British intelligence. Both these latter couples, although their circumstances and histories differed, had left-wing social and political beliefs.

They were all kind to me. No one made the least effort to press me to adopt their views of life and society—almost certainly because no one took me seriously as a political person.

Nan, a vicar's daughter, and Ted, a Welshman, lived in Wandsworth, a working-class district in the city. Nan was a widow. Her husband, George, had volunteered for the Republican forces in the Spanish Civil War and had been killed in the battle of the Ebro River. She had had two children with him, Martin and Frances, who lived with her and Ted in a bleak housing unit that had been thrown up, it seemed to me, overnight, after a bombing raid had destroyed whatever building had been there.

The flat was skimpy, meagerly furnished. A narrow stairway led from the living room to two tiny bedrooms on the second floor, in one of which I slept.

I was fond of Nan and of her son, fourteen-year-old Martin, and his younger sister, Frances, but I had mixed feelings about Ted, who was employed by a London gasworks. He was dry and laconic with me. He rarely spoke to Nan in my presence, as though their relationship were a secret.

Fifty-seven years later, I can still catch a glimpse of Frances through the half-opened door of the bathroom, sitting in a few inches of water in a small tub. She is fleshy and pink and holds a scrap of soap in her plump pretty upheld hands as though she has just fished it out of the water. She smiles faintly at something I am saying as I pass by on my way to the kitchen.

Most of the year the children were away attending Summerhill, an experimental school in the south of England (I'm not sure when the word *progressive* made its way into the language). It was founded and run by a man, A. S. Neill, who was referred to as Neill by Frances and Martin. Although *run* may not be the exact word since, I gathered, the students did much as they pleased in the way of classes and subjects.

I got a job at the London office of 20th Century-Fox, where I worked briefly as a reader of manuscripts, looking for ones I thought had film potential. But I found steadier work with Victor Gollancz, reading manuscripts for a guinea or two each. He'd hired me not only because he'd known my father when Daddy lived in England but because his regular and longtime reader had been assaulted by an unhinged Irishman whose stories about the Ulster Legends and Cuchulainn she'd rejected after reading the opening section.

Somehow the Irishman had learned her name, waited until she was on her way home, and sent her to the hospital with broken ribs and a bruised face. She was not expected to return to the Gollancz offices for six weeks. After telling me this, Victor warned me not to speak to anyone about where and in what capacity I was employed.

One afternoon, I was alone in the Wandsworth flat, reading a manuscript, when there was a sharp knock on the front door. I looked through the mail slot, and saw dark cloth. I opened the door with my gut clenched. A bobby towered over me, or maybe it was only his helmet that made it seem so. He touched it with two fingers, addressed me as *miss,* and asked me if I held a work permit. I shook my head no. He said I'd need to come to the police station with him.

Once there, I filled out a form that required me to swear not to take employment that a British citizen could do and, further, to work only at part-time jobs. I had heard that one needed a work permit but had not taken the requirement seriously. Perhaps it was myself I did not take seriously. For a minute I grasped at the shadowy nature of reality; of how one moves through it like a mist, forever thinking of what comes next and how impalpable the present is.

I made my way back to Wandsworth chastened. The housing unit was four stories high, and on every floor it had open corridors that ran in front of the flats for the length of the building.

Approaching dusk had nearly darkened the steps I climbed. I held the work permit in my hand, consoled by its meaning: The government protected its citizens and took my presence in England seriously.

I RODE THE NUMBER 19 BUS TO CHELSEA, WHERE MY father's friend, Benn Levy, lived on Old Church Street in a house designed by the well-known architect Marcel Breuer. Benn was married to an American actress, Constance Cummings, whom he always addressed by her last name. I was to spend a few weeks with them.

Benn was a playwright and a Labour Member of Parliament. The first meant something to me, the second not much. I was ignorant of most of the history of Parliament, although at least aware of its division into the House of Lords and the House of Commons.

The Labour Party leader Aneurin Bevan made an evening visit to Benn while I was there. In the brief moment of introduction, before I excused myself from the room, I was aware of a gray presence who looked at me intently but with blank eyes. He had two shorter men with him who didn't remove their raincoats, at least not while I was in the room.

I had been given a small bedroom on the first floor, tucked in

behind a staircase, ultramodern for those days, that seemed to float upward, an impression enhanced by the open space at the back of each step.

Until I spent time in the Levy home, the places people inhabited had not figured in my judgment of them. I had been only conscious of my own comfort or discomfort: so-and-so's place was a misery, another's was big and furnished like a store.

It was the Breuer-designed house on Church Street that made me reflect for the first time on the settings of rich people I had met, or observed in films, and their concern about the effect of their style on others, subtly changing over time into what I thought was an insane confidence that the objects with which they surrounded themselves reflected their praiseworthy character, not the ease with which they spent money.

The airy stairway led me to think of the circular link between ground and pit at the Catskill resort where I had worked, of subway steps with common daily life ground into them and cement platforms marked with blotches of flattened chewing gum, and of the narrow staircase at Nan's Wandsworth housing development, and how taste, pretense, avarice, and necessity were expressed through them all.

On my first morning at the Levys, I was awakened by a knock on the door, followed by the entrance of a servant carrying a tray holding tea, toast, and a dried fish on a plate. It resembled a mummy; I managed a small bite before abandoning it.

SHARING THE VAST LAWN AND GARDENS WITH BENN AND Cummings was another architect-designed house owned by a publisher, Dennis Cohen, and his American wife, Kay. Dennis reminded me of George Arliss, an elderly actor of the period. Kay was decades younger and had been an American chorus girl. But now, Benn told me, she was studying medicine to become a doctor. In 1946, there were few women doctors in London.

From the beginning of my stay, Benn spoke to me with a kind of intimacy, both avuncular and loverlike. He had an easy, somewhat sweet way about him. Once he came into an upstairs bathroom while I was washing my underwear in a sink. He lingered in the doorway, a half smile on his face, and said, "Washing out your smalls, are you?" I observed this charming, vaguely seductive manner in his conversations with women of any age. During a party at his house, he sat at the piano and played and sang a music-hall tune, "Hard-hearted Hannah," with great aplomb.

When Benn went away for a few days, Cummings told me he'd gone to Ireland with Larry Olivier for "a decent English breakfast." I was surprised to learn that Laurence Olivier actually ate breakfast; he seemed to me one of the immortals who never needed food.

The Levys belonged to a London Key Club, through which it was possible for them to procure fresh fruit and vegetables, hard to come by in those days of some rationing and much scarcity.

They lived in style, surrounded by costly but neutral furniture and furnishings that didn't stay the eye. Benn was playful; they were both captious at times, but it was Cummings who frightened me by her tone of voice. It was moderate, without depth, cool.

It was in that tone that she told me over a Soho lunch about the death of a Hollywood screenwriter, Vincent Lawrence. He was another friend of my father's and had written plays before he went to California. I had loved Vin, partly for his protective impulses toward me, and stopped eating. Cummings continued on to speak of some trivial matter to a friend of hers who was with us.

One evening she took me backstage after we'd seen a play about the troubles of middle-class marriage. Cummings and the cast members were all speaking about the *servant problem* in voices that I judged to be silly and affected, as they all tried to outdo one another with examples of staff slovenliness and ineptitude. It was a recent difficulty for those who could afford servants. Factory work had given people choices, a taste of freedom from being in service.

I felt more at ease with Kay Cohen, who invited me to a dinner party one evening. I spent the afternoon in a movie theater watching Carl Dreyer's *Day of Wrath.* My mind was full of its drifting beauty and its savagery. As I walked to Chelsea in the gray dusk, on the gray streets, I was followed by a small sinister-looking man in a cap. London wasn't as crowded as it has become, and we were alone except for a hurrying figure or two. He hung back, came close, once went ahead of me on some steps, and turned to stare down at me crazily like a rat in a tree. I ran past him, still in the grip of the film's menace, but he only grinned at me. He had won! Then he suddenly skittered away.

Several hours later, I went to the Cohens' opulent home. Dennis and Kay and their guests talked quietly in the living room; I guessed the slow pace of their words was out of respect

for Dennis's advanced age but I was mistaken. Most formal dinner parties, as I learned in later years, began in such a way, and
the slowness could usually be accounted for by the contest—
between avidity for company and food and boredom with the
same—being waged in each guest. During an unexpected
silence, I mentioned having seen the Dreyer film earlier that
afternoon. Encouraged by their attention, I told the story of
Day of Wrath with an intensity that later mortified me, especially when Dennis commented, "I simply can't bear films in
which doomed young couples walk through fields holding
hands," in the most lordly accent and emphasis I'd heard since
I'd come to England.

Kay spoke up at once. "*Really,* Dennis," she said, in a critical
voice that helped to salve my wounded feelings.

While I was living in Chelsea, I got a few modeling jobs
with the British version of *Harper's Bazaar* that didn't interfere
with my work for Gollancz. During our lunch break, in a loft with
other models, I ate fish and chips wrapped in newspaper brought
on the run to us by thin young boys.

Then I was hired by a British peer for his small news service.
I was to be sent first to Paris and then to Warsaw. It was my last
job in England—and, as it turned out, in Europe.

Kay loaned me a fur-lined tweed coat which I made use of
that winter in Paris, where I was to spend a month or so, and
then in Warsaw for the first elections since the end of the war.
There the coat, a piece of borrowed finery indeed, saved my life.

When I returned to England before going on to Poland, I
learned from Benn that Kay had finished medical school and

gone to Switzerland for a skiing holiday. One early morning, in the chalet where she was staying, she killed herself. By what means I never heard, or for what reason.

WHILE I WAS STILL LIVING WITH BENN AND CUMMINGS, I spent an evening with a friend, Derek, at Beatrix Lehmann's flat on the banks of the Thames. We arrived just as she put on a record. She whispered to us that it was Benjamin Britten's song cycle sung by Peter Pears. The songs included a poem by William Blake, "O Rose, Thou Art Sick," and a fourteenth-century dirge, "This Ae Night." Even as I heard it, I was haunted—and I am still—by the piercing thorn of Peter Pears's voice and the severe and unfamiliar fourteenth-century English words.

Beatrix was an actress. Her brother John, poet and essayist, was the editor of a then well-known fiction magazine. The third member of the family was the novelist Rosamund Lehmann.

Beatrix had just returned from a tour with an acting company in Germany. They went to cities where British troops were stationed, transported from place to place by a tour bus.

In the ruins of Berlin, she had seen, she swore, a small dusty mongrel emerge from a massive pile of fire-blackened stone and brick and hurl itself under the bus wheels.

She looked at me deeply. "Suicide of a Berlin dog," she intoned.

The dirge I had heard, the tale of the mongrel, and the intense atmosphere in the room filled me with a mysterious happiness, an anticipation of my life to come.

. . .

MY LAST TWO WEEKS IN LONDON WERE SPENT IN ST. JOHN'S
Wood with a journalist, Claude, and his wife, Pat, an Irish
princess without a real tooth in her mouth.

She had spent her childhood in the north of Ireland in a castle.
It was dark, dank, and bleak. Her family couldn't afford to send
her to a dentist and her second teeth had rotted away. But she was
handsome and charming and her false teeth gleamed bravely
because she smiled so often. Claude had worked for *The* (London)
Times for years. During the war, he had been dropped by para-
chute several times to meet with former town officials and resistance people in occupied France and Belgium. After the war he
went to work for *The Daily Worker,* the Communist newspaper.

Pat and Claude had met for the first time at a dinner party.
They were married to other people but they fell in love at once,
Pat told me. She had some money and she made arrangements to
take Claude, a heavy drinker, on an African safari. He returned a
sober man. There had been no pubs along their route.

Claude showed me a postcard the newspaper had received
from George Bernard Shaw. It was an apology of sorts for the
errors in an article Shaw had written for them. "Shaw at 90!" it
read. "What a pity!" I touched his signature as though it had
been his face.

Claude was a storyteller as my father had been. One story concerned his efforts to keep all the addresses and resistance names
of the people he met as a war correspondent for *The Times.* He
lost notebook after notebook. At last he resorted to covering his
study walls with the names of European officials, underground

leaders, and journalists, the last unemployed because of the German occupation. Toward the end of the Second World War, however, a V-2 rocket destroyed two flats and Claude's study. Fortunately, both Pat and he were out when the rocket shattered his extended address book.

Another tale concerned an old man who survived a rocket attack in London. He was discovered by air wardens, shielded by a cocoon of rubble, sitting in his bathtub. "All I did was pull the plug to let out the water," he explained defensively to his rescuers. I heard the same story from someone else after Claude had told it to me, so I concluded it was apocryphal.

One Saturday afternoon, Pat took me to a matinee at the Old Vic to see Laurence Olivier in a production of *King Lear*. We had seats in the front row, so when old Lear was sheltering on the blasted heath with Poor Tom, I could glimpse, just behind the curtain, a stagehand beating a metal sheet to simulate thunder. Rather than reducing the illusion of the play, the sight increased it for me.

During the lengthy intermission, I heard the clatter of china and turned in my seat to see ushers carrying trays, moving quickly along the aisles. We were going to be served tea. Perhaps the actors backstage also had a tea break.

ONE MORNING DURING THE DAYS I SPENT WITH PAT AND Claude, as I walked along a sidewalk next to Hyde Park to pick up a manuscript from Gollancz, work I did now and then after I'd been hired by the British peer, a strange sight met my eyes. It was as though Birnum Wood had risen next to the park and was moving toward me on the pavement: a clump of men were carrying and pushing a drunken Winston Churchill. Not only was he weeping but mascara was puddling under his eyes before it ran down his plump cheeks. Claude told me later that Churchill's eyelashes were so light he always wore mascara for filmed interviews. But he said nothing about the noble statesman's penchant for alcohol.

I MET WITH THE PEER, SIR ANDREW, THE NEXT MORNING. The other people who worked for him, he had explained, had private incomes to support them, along with the very small salaries he was able to offer. He might, he said, pay me a bit more. He told me I was to attend the peace conference that was taking place at the Palais du Luxembourg. "And be sure to make friends with the labor attaché at the American embassy," he added. He handed me a train ticket for my passage to France, a third-class seat on the Flèche d'Or that would deposit me in Paris.

Sir Andrew, I found, was a private person. What little I knew about him, beside what I could see—the same thick black wool suit he had worn during my first interview with him; the Sweet Caporals he smoked, flicking ashes about himself; his small features crowded into a large expanse of face; lots of dull black hair—was that he was well-off, strong in his championing of the rights of labor, and wanted to spend his pounds and shillings on a news service with a very different political emphasis from Reuters.

Some nerve! I told myself silently, to imagine he could compete with such a famed service.

PARIS

A year and a half after the end of the war and the German occupation, Paris was muted and looked bruised and forlorn. Everywhere I went, I sensed the tracks of the wolf that had tried to devour the city. But Paris proved inedible, as it had been ever since its tribal beginnings on an island in the Seine, the Ile de la Cité.

I stood on the Champs-Elysées, down which the black-booted Nazis had marched, some with reverence and cultural piety, I had heard, some triumphant, some astonished that they should be in command of the City of Light. But there was little brightness in 1946, except at sunset on a fair day when the last of the sun's rays struck the roof of Sacré-Coeur and the flying buttresses of Notre-Dame and the spindle top of the Eiffel

Tower; except in the bright scarves of the Frenchwomen who walked swiftly and insouciantly as they went about their daily tasks and errands to the baker, the grocer, the butcher, and the open markets that had begun that year to display their wares. Perhaps the women were hoping to find their former lives among the stalls. But though there was no bomb damage, as there had been in London, the old life of Paris was gone.

When I returned as a tourist decades later, the stairs and corridors of the Louvre flowed with foreign visitors. But in 1946, I was nearly alone in the museum except for a drunken elderly custodian, whose eyes swam toward me every so often, suspicion of me evident in his downturned lips and lifted eyebrows, as though I might try to steal the *Mona Lisa,* then on the ground floor, or *The Winged Victory of Samothrace,* standing at the top of a long flight of white marble steps.

I found a pension on the rue de Longchamp and made arrangements for a room. It was cheerless, shabby, and barely heated.

In the evenings I sometimes played bridge with other boarders. I always had the same partner, who seemed determined to keep me seated opposite her and requested me, in an ironic voice, to call her *madame.* I couldn't imagine what her irony was about, unless she judged me to be a callous American or unless it expressed her attitude toward life itself. Then I saw one evening, as she dealt the cards, the faded blue tattoo of a number on the inside of her wrist. It was the first time I saw such a mark, although it was not the last. She was in her thirties, she told me, but looked at least a decade older.

She didn't eat her meals on the dishes provided by the pension but transferred the food to a mess kit she had been issued in Dachau—the concentration camp where she had been a prisoner for thirteen months—and ate it hastily with a spoon as though she expected it to be snatched away at any second. She was the only boarder who tied a string around her bottle of wine because, she told me, if someone else in the pension drank from it, she wanted to know. Just that. To know.

From the year I had spent in a Montreal boarding school, I recalled the beautiful French words for card suits: *carreau, pique, coeur, trèfle.* But I played erratically, too excited, unable to concentrate on the cards, made restless by the city, by my partner's past, by all the people I had met and would meet. We rarely won.

She appeared to grieve as if more than a game of cards had been at stake. When I bade her good night, she would barely respond as she sat slumped in a chair, her eyes shut.

When I had a few francs, I spent them at a café on the Place de Longchamps, a block or so from my pension, where I could order a glass of Beaujolais and a plate of string beans in vinaigrette for the equivalent of fifteen cents. At the lunch hour I could see, through large clear windows, people strolling along streets and sidewalks, carrying long narrow baguettes. One end of the loaf was always missing, bitten off and eaten by its purchaser, who wanted the pleasure of its freshness or simply because to do so was a Parisian habit.

Every few days I would mail off a story to the London wire service. Its budget, I had been informed by Sir Andrew, was too low to permit the use of telephones. What expenses he would cover were only for emergencies he didn't enumerate. In any event, my stories tended toward the picturesque rather than the newsworthy.

The first time I visited the labor attaché at the American embassy, one of my sources for slow news, I was struck by the radiance of the sunlight streaming through the windows behind his desk, which cast everything else, including the attaché, into the shade. It was only when he strode to the rear of the room that I was able to see him. He was tall and lanky and not quite young, I judged. He reached into a file cabinet and, from an empty space at its back, lifted out a carton of cigarettes that he carried back to his desk. He held out the carton to me, saying "Good morning" at the same time.

Cigarettes were quite as valuable as money in 1946. One could smoke a few and sell the rest on a flourishing black market.

All I recall from the humdrum conversation was his invitation to me to accompany him and a few friends who planned a trip to the south of France the coming weekend.

No, thank you, I replied, though I was tempted by the resonance of the names of the areas and villages—the Rhône Valley, Saint-Emilion, Saint-Remy, Arles, the Camargue—he planned to visit.

A few days later, I met and interviewed a Corsican politician whose exploits in the Resistance were the subject of a cartoon strip sold in all the kiosks of Paris. His name was Jean-Claude. He was tall and slim, dark-haired, somber-looking, in his early thirties. We fell in love.

In the last months of the war, when she was in her seventh month of pregnancy, his wife had been captured by the Gestapo. To force her to reveal his whereabouts, she was beaten with a rubber truncheon on every part of her body. Ultimately, she was released although she had given nothing away. The baby, a boy, was born unharmed.

In the shadow of his wife's monumental heroism and loyalty, there was little enough we could say to each other or do. There was no future, only the past. We told each other our histories, our breaths mingling, as we rode the Metro under all of Paris. Sometimes he smoked the English cigarettes he preferred to the strong French tobacco. We met at odd hours in small dark bistros where we drank harsh red wine. We made quick, intense love in dark courtyards, her bravery never far from our minds. Once, we were seen embracing against a wall. From his second-floor window, a heavy-set elderly man called out, *"Honteux!"* I wept from embarrassment. Jean-Claude tried to comfort me. It was all hopeless.

Jean-Claude had to return to Corsica for a week. The evening he told me about the trip, gripping my hand in his while he spoke, it was as if our flesh knew a second before we did that we would not see each other again. We withdrew our hands. We parted outside the café where we had met, and, walking away from each other on a lamplit sidewalk, we both turned at the same instant to look back. His face was shadowed, as mine must have been, as our faces would be in memory. And I felt, along with a bitter rue I could nearly taste, an unexpected relief, as one does after high emotions, a small death, a reminder that one is finally alone.

...

ONE EVENING, THE HUSBAND OF A COUPLE I HAD INTER-
viewed for the news service picked me up in his car at the pension and drove me to their apartment in the Marais to have
dinner with them. The traffic was sparse. As we drove, he told
me the sheepskin jacket he was wearing had kept him warm the
three years he had spent in a concentration camp. The jacket
had holes at each elbow and seemed to me the brown carcass of
an animal that had fought in vain for its life.

He hadn't been worked to death or gassed. He was a medical
doctor and of use to the camp administration. When he pro-
nounced the word *administration* I imagined I saw his concentration-camp face for an instant in the dashboard light. Then he
regained his friendly expression.

The large bourgeois flat faced a shadowed interior courtyard.
Dinner had many courses, perhaps to make up for the tiny por-
tions. It ended with unexpected opulence, a great wheel of
Roquefort cheese from which his wife cut thin slices, their
blue-veined surfaces resembling a city map of streets.

At some point, the conversation turned to *les mutilés*. I was
startled to learn that in French it meant *the wounded*. *Mutilated*
has a powerful sense of malice aforethought, the infliction on
another of savagery and torture. Though the war had ended a
year earlier, the trains still returned these soldiers to Paris.
After that evening, I watched for them, walking with canes or
splints or bandages wrapped around their heads like turbans.
For a few days, the English meaning of the word refused to give
way to the French.

I had occasion to take a taxi somewhere soon after my dinner in the Marais. Once he knew I was American, the driver told me two stories in a voice filled with animus. *Grosses enfants* he called the American soldiers stationed in France just after the war, as a preface to describing to me how they threw hand grenades at barns or farmhouses from their jeeps as they drove aimlessly about the countryside of France, indifferent to the lives of those within. He may have sensed my disbelief because he amended his tale by adding that the soldiers might have judged the farmhouses deserted.

The second story concerned a stranded American climber in the Alps. The U.S. Army moved a trainful of GIs to the base of the mountain, along with a restaurant car and medical personnel. Meanwhile, a lone Swiss had gone up the mountain, rescued the climber, and brought him down to safety.

IN EARLY NOVEMBER, SEVERAL JOURNALISTS, I AMONG THEM, were chosen to take a trip by train to the northwest coast of France. We were to spend one night at Mont-Saint-Michel and then go south to Saint-Malo and Dinan, everything paid for by the government.

A dozen or so of us boarded a one-car train, crates of champagne stacked up on the back platform rattling as the train moved out of the station. On board were three Russians, two guarding a third, the son of the Marshal Zhukov who had defeated the Germans at Stalingrad and lifted the siege of Leningrad in 1944. The son was tall and homely. His skin was

khaki-colored, and whenever our glances crossed, he grinned hugely and waved, even though I was sitting nearby. It was an odd sight to see his large hand bending its fingers, the cuff of his uniform unmoving as though he were made of cement.

There were a few Americans, among whom was Nick, a United Press journalist I had become friendly with, several English people, and a boy of nineteen or so whose pants, I noticed, were held at his waist by a large safety pin. His jacket was far too thin for the cold weather. His expression was one of sullen disregard for the rest of us; I had the sense it was a perpetual expression except when he slept, always false, always provocative, although he appeared too weak to provoke anyone.

Nick informed me that the boy had been a member of a fascist youth organization in Hungary. How he'd made his way from there to Paris and the peace conference and then onto this train, Nick couldn't explain.

We spent our first night at La Mère Poularde, an inn with a restaurant on the main street of Mont-Saint-Michel. The restaurant's specialty was a seemingly endless variety of omelets cooked over a narrow stone trench of flame in a kitchen as large as the dining room. But unlike the latter, it had a sixteenth-century look, an impression strengthened by the cook's long muslin dress and head wrap and the massive wooden door behind her, with its ponderous, regal iron hardware. In the dining room were several tables, each with a candle in a glass cup, and one wall of glass behind which stood two thick-trunked living trees in leaf.

Nick, sitting across from me, told a story about a man who had gone to a New Jersey airport, chosen a ramp, and run down it, flapping his arms, to fly to the Paris peace conference, where he intended to say a few stern words to the delegates. Everyone who understood English laughed except the fascist youth and Zhukov's son, both of whom ate steadily, not looking up at anyone.

I remembered the narrow street outside, curving like a nautilus shell on its way up to the eighth-century abbey, which we had toured earlier that day. I had passed an oubliette, a cell in the ground. Weeds grew around its iron grill. Prisoners inside it would have had to have crouched; the idea was harrowing, and I felt a moment of claustrophobia when I thought of soft human flesh being stuffed into such a narrow burrow for months and years.

The entrance to the fortresslike abbey had been shrouded in darkness. I stood at the great doors watching as visitors took careful steps into the interior, just as I had seen local people do. The French of Mont-Saint-Michel have gathered seaweed from the sea shallows and learned over generations to avoid the patches of quicksand for which that part of the coast is known.

After dinner, I made my way back to the abbey. I reached the great black-spired hulk and realized the Hungarian boy was a few yards behind me. I turned to see him. He stood, unmoving, his head bent, his hands in his trouser pockets. I walked to the rocky outcrop and he followed me, always maintaining the same distance between us. I saw how his torn shirt collar played against his cheek. He began to speak, not with me but at me, in his limping French. I understood enough of what the wind left of his words to realize he was talking about his short past, the excitement in his voice quickened, I guessed, by the blowing wind and the height we stood upon and the starlight glinting on the surface of the water far below.

He didn't speak of Jews or Gypsies or homosexuals but only of executions he had witnessed, as if they had been the romance of his life, but it was all over now; he had no place to go, no place to be. He didn't care what happened to him.

I pitied him for his starved look, for his youth. But I hated him too. When he grew silent, I walked away, down the long winding street, back to the inn.

THE TIDE WAS LOW WHEN WE BOARDED THE SMALL BUSES TO return to the mainland, where our train awaited us.

In Saint-Malo, the mayor had given us an afternoon party in a small villa on a bluff overlooking the sea. A German block-house rose on the beach, and I stood in it for a few minutes, staring at the wall I faced. It was covered with graffiti in German and French. An empty blue pack of Gaulois lay crumpled on the cement floor, along with debris left by high tides.

Chilled to the bone by the sea wind, as well as by memories not my own, perhaps from war movies I'd seen, I returned to the villa, where a man was waiting for me at the salt-air-ravaged hedgerow.

"There's someone who would like to speak to you," he said, waving at a bit of cultivated ground just behind him. "He'd like to ask you a few questions about your country."

I walked into the autumnal garden. Leaning on a birdbath was a short man with one eye that wandered. He wore glasses.

There were thawing fragments of dirty ice in the birdbath. I noticed his ungloved left hand clutching its rim. During our brief conversation, it seemed to me he had always looked the same age.

He grew aware at last that I was shivering and led me back into the living room of the villa. I heard his name murmured by someone, Jean-Paul Sartre. I had heard of him, vaguely, and I cursed myself for foolishness, recalling how knowledgeably I had spoken of the United States—especially California, about which he'd asked me many questions—when in fact I was so ignorant.

Nick rolled his eyes when I described to him how I had held forth to Sartre. "Him big cheese in some circles," he commented.

Marshal Zhukov's son—I've forgotten his first name— strode in a military fashion across the room to me, his bodyguards, resembling fire hydrants, striving to keep up with him on their short stubby legs. Bowing too often, Zhukov invited me to visit him in Moscow, where he then lived. I smiled and gave him an elaborate refusal, which he mistook, I think, for yes. Then I bowed and he bowed, and the whole thing became a tangle through which I finally made my escape.

I RETURNED TO PARIS, MY WORK DONE, SLIGHT THOUGH IT had been.

I said adieu to a woman friend, Lucienne. She stood on the pavement beside a grand boulevard, her beret askew from our embrace a second earlier. I was returning to London to be reassigned to Poland. On my last evening in Paris, I took a walk on the Left Bank. The streets were nearly empty as I neared the café Les Deux Magots.

Suddenly from out of the shadows a figure approached me. The weak streetlamp made her hair a halo. She was carrying in one hand a glass of white wine.

It was Maggie, whom I'd last seen in New York City in a sublet on the East Side, when she gave me the names of two families I had stayed with in London. She had been holding a cocktail glass then, with the remains of a martini in it. I had stopped by to see her the day before she was to return to her home in London. Strewn around her had been opened boxes of clothes and handbags and shoes. She was smiling, her handsome face triumphant yet rueful, as she told me how she had charged everything—she gestured toward the loot around us— and was taking it home with her and, yes, she was skipping out on the bill that would come at the end of the month. She laughed and toasted the air and drank down the rest of the martini.

The world was different then in so many significant or trivial ways. One was how easily you could escape your bills if you left the country where you owed them. She had been so merry and winsome that day, her blond curls framing her face, drinking gin, her stolen goods spread on furniture and tables about the room. Somehow she managed to look sleek and disheveled at the same time.

But for me the stealing had been shocking, and my face must have shown it.

"Don't think about it for another second," she said. "Pretend I paid cash." But I couldn't not think about it.

Now she was walking toward me, looking like a tarnished angel, from the Deux Magots. She said she'd spotted me from a window in the café. She didn't ask me one question about why I was in Paris.

I had first met her in New York City among a group of Communist sympathizers, otherwise known then as fellow travelers. There had been rumors that she was employed as a spy by British intelligence. It seemed the height of sophistication in those days—to meet a beautiful looter, a reputed British agent, in a Paris street at night, with a glass of wine in her hand.

I swallowed the memory of what she had done and what she might be doing and, as she held it out, took the wineglass from her hand and drank what was left.

LONDON AGAIN

I returned to London at the end of November. The city streets were dank, and in daylight they looked grimy and desolate. But at night the windows of flats glittered like the lights of a ship across black water and gave me an impression of watery motion. After years of a blackout I had only heard about, the lights felt celebratory.

Even streetlamps joined the party, glimmering like reflections in ponds. In the frequent late-autumn fog, everything appeared to float a foot above the ground: churches, houses, people.

My employer and I met for lunch at the Cheshire Cheese.

"Samuel Johnson is said to have dined here frequently," Sir Andrew whispered to me. I had to lean across the table to catch his words.

He was sending me to Prague by air, but I would have to take the train from there to Warsaw, my ultimate destination. In Prague, I would spend a few hours with a Czech journalist he had met once or twice in London.

"He's married to an Englishwoman whose name eludes me. Well, you'll only be spending a few hours with him; you don't have to know her name." He frowned down at his plate and then continued reluctantly, as though begrudging me the information. "His first wife was killed by the Nazis. They were both extremely political, of course, though I hear from a fellow at Reuters that Jan is awfully changed since the war and his—er, losses." He handed me a small card. "I've written out his last name phonetically so you can pronounce it, should he not show up at the airport. In that case, perhaps you could find your way to his digs."

I noticed the dirty edges of his cuffs and how dandruff spotted the shoulders of his dark suit. I had ordered a plowman's lunch, as it was called in the Cheshire Cheese, and had been unable to finish it.

"Then you will continue on to Warsaw on the train that leaves Prague around midnight," he went on. "First the Nazis occupied Warsaw, then the Russians. Now the Poles will be having their first election. Ah, well, you won't be covering *that* directly, but send me a few stories about it and other aspects of life as it's lived among the ruins. In the States, I believe they're called human-interest or local-color features.

"In Warsaw, you can add your material to that of Desmond Birch, who writes for a British agricultural journal, or else to Mary Burke's; she writes for the *Irish Times*. Also, you can mail features to me directly—an interview with an architect, for example, who has plans for the rebuilding of the city, subjects of interest to readers who are not as interested in news stories as they are in life stories. Birch and Burke are staying at the Polonia Hotel, a few yards from where you'll be staying. Oh, my dear!" he exclaimed suddenly, but with no change in his tone of voice. "Warsaw is utterly destroyed. To speak of hotels means only three. A fourth is being erected even as we sit here, to accommodate the new members, delegates perhaps to the Polish Parliament, who will arrive before the December election. I think it will be sufficiently completed for you to stay there on your first night in the city."

He said the last words with a faint smile. I interpreted it as meaning he was willing to spend more money than he usually did on my first night's accommodation in Warsaw.

"After that, you will move to the Centralny, a small place but right in the middle of things. I doubt you'll have any trouble—except for the cold, of course."

"It couldn't be colder than Paris," I said.

"Oh, yes, it can and will be. Don't forget, it's Eastern Europe."

"There were days in Paris when I didn't want to leave the Metro because it was the warmest place I knew. I got to know some people on the trains who had the same idea."

He seemed not to have taken in my words. "Awful conditions in Poland, as I said. I warn you: even though some food is on the ration here in England, this is a tropical heaven compared to Warsaw. I would think over this trip if I were you. You aren't required to go. I can give you assignments in London: interviews with the striking miners, and with a publisher or two—Victor, who employed you and whom I know; Dennis Cohen, also an acquaintance of mine—subjects like that."

For an instant he looked nettled as though he didn't like the idea of my interviewing other publishers. He sighed and looked at me directly. "Will you want coffee?" he asked. "It will be dreadful. I believe it's partly made with chicory."

"No, thank you. I've had enough of everything."

"You've not finished your cheese," he said.

"I'm full, Sir Andrew."

"Mustn't waste," he said. He reached across the table, gathered up the scraps of cheese on my plate with his long bony fingers, and swallowed the scraps in two gulps, his prominent Adam's apple rippling.

For a peer, he didn't look so well fed.

I TOOK THE TUBE TO WANDSWORTH. IT WAS THE WEEKEND SO I guessed Nan and Ted would be at home. When I arrived, Ted was kneeling on the floor of the open corridor to lay the last section of a miniature railroad track. He waved to me. "Watch your step!" he warned. At that moment Nan appeared, emerging from their flat carrying a steam locomotive. She placed it down on the track. Frances, and Martin whose birthday present the train was, came to stand in the doorway, their faces lightened and happy for the moment. They shivered in the cold air.

Ted had found the imposing toy locomotive in a London

junk shop and worked on it for weeks, restoring it to its original glory. It gleamed in the pale afternoon light, oiled and powerful-looking, small though it was. Now it emitted steam and a loud triumphant hoot. We all cheered and applauded as the locomotive went chugging down the tracks, its large side wheels turning.

I parted from them. Their faces, as I imagined mine was, were softened with delight, with foolish, affectionate smiles—we were still imagining the train steaming on its way, moments free of the tensions that turn the wheels of daily life.

I MADE MY WAY TO CHELSEA TO VISIT BENN AND CUMMINGS but they were not home; he had gone to Ireland again, and she was in a matinee performance of a West End play. Only the maid, who had served me the desiccated herring, came to the door.

Then I rang the door of the flat in St. John's Wood. There was no answer.

I looked up and down the sidewalk. It was the first time I had had time on my hands since I'd come to Europe. I had nothing to do. I started in one direction with a stride full of intention but almost at once realized I didn't have one. So I stood motionless in the dying light of a winter afternoon in northern Europe, feeling the unfamiliar weight of the present moment before time moved me on. I found myself standing in front of one of London's most well-known music halls. I bought a ticket after a few moments of listening to a street musician play a noisy tune on a trumpet.

I recall a female singer, blond, in her middle years, with a robust, rather tuneless voice. But most vividly I remember Bud Flanagan. He was, I think, a member of a troupe called the Crazy Gang.

The various sets on stage were drawn back like curtains, all the way to the first. A small rotund figure wearing a peculiar hat was slowly walking toward the front of the stage, through the edges of set after set, looming larger every moment, until the audience was rocking with recognition and laughter.

Bud was smoking a cigar, its smoke trailing behind him. He stood there scowling for a long moment, then removed the cigar from his mouth.

"What the hell are you all laughin' at?" he asked.

AFTER THE MUSIC HALL, I WENT TO RED LION SQUARE FOR A reason I don't recollect. There was a thick fog and, ribboned through it, the red lights of a pub. Music from a radio wafted over the square. I was at the center of the world. I was twenty-three years old. Then I wondered if any place where a person stood did not seem to be the center.

The next afternoon, I took the plane for Prague.

SMILE

On a darkening early December afternoon in 1946, I arrived from London at the Prague airport in a small passenger plane that flew on toward Warsaw, its ultimate destination. It was carrying journalists who worked for big wire services or newspapers, unlike myself, a stringer who was worth plane fare only as far as Prague. Toward midnight of that day, I would have to take a train the rest of the way to the Polish capital.

In the nearly empty airport, I saw a small neat-looking man with fair crimped hair who was evidently looking for me. We met; we shook hands. He was Jan. The gaze he fixed on me was steady and impassive; his lips were faintly widened in a half smile that didn't leave his face during the hours I spent with him and his wife, Rose. Except when he was drinking tea, of course.

We took a bus to the city. At some point, I had an impression that his eyes were golden, but it was only a passing effect from the headlights of the one car we passed on the narrow road. I suppose his eyes were hazel.

He told me he had recently married Rose, an English-woman, who worked for a postwar refugee organization. It was she who welcomed me into their small flat in a building so cheaply and recently erected that it still smelled dankly of fresh plaster. She had made us tea, saying we must be frozen by that horrid wind that always sprang up toward the end of the day in the city of Prague. Beyond the two small windows of the living room, it was now black. She had bought a little cake and made a few coarse-looking sandwiches. "The bread," she remarked, shrugging in a show of patient helplessness. Another thing to be borne as part of postwar life in Central Europe.

I had an impression she didn't stop talking during the hours I spent in the flat, except when I interrupted her with questions of an ordinary sort. I didn't care what she answered. I wanted to break the awful continuity of her bright, implacably cheer-ful voice that gave the same weight to whatever subject she brought up.

I knew so little, and the little I did know, I didn't under-stand. My ravenous interest in those days was aroused by any-thing.

Jan watched Rose's every move, the half smile fixed on his face. I slowly recognized in him an underlying desperation. Later, when we were on the trolley to the station, when he spoke to me of the fate of his family during the Nazi occupation of Czechoslovakia, I was unable to take in the meaning of his story except suddenly, and then for only a few seconds at a time. When I did, it was as though I grasped broken glass in my hand.

Rose's avalanche of words slackened when she turned on their small radio, already tuned to an English news program. She sat down to listen. I realized she had been in constant motion since I'd arrived at the flat. Now she slipped her hands beneath her apron as though they were cold. I thought I could see her prominent knuckles through the thin cloth. But by then, it was time to leave.

Jan had pressed his cheek against hers when we arrived, and he did the same when we left. I turned away from them. The slow pressing of flesh against flesh was more intimate to me than a passionate kiss would have been.

We walked several blocks in the shadowed gloom of Prague, the sidewalk lit fitfully by pools of light at the bottom of the few working streetlamps, until we heard the rumble of an approaching trolley. It halted for us, and we climbed up the narrow steps. Inside, a few women sat stolidly on slatted seats. Some stared at the floor; others looked out of dusty windows. One, wearing a babushka, fell asleep just as we passed the Charles Bridge.

Jan began to talk in a composed voice about his ten-year-old twin girls. I may have missed a few words because of the clamor of the trolley.

The twins had been taken to a camp run by Josef Mengele. Both had perished during something called an experiment by Dr. Mengele. Jan's wife had died of starvation and despair in a concentration camp east of Prague. He himself had spent years

in a different camp. No, he replied to my question, he wasn't a Jew, only political.

He pressed my arm and nodded at a large building across the street. It was the railroad station.

There wasn't any traffic as we crossed the broad street. In the dim station, I had a moment of fear and didn't want to leave Jan's side. He took my arm then and pressed me forward to the waiting train, its engine sending out white plumes of steam. As we stood at the foot of the black metal steps, he told me his second story.

"A professor I once knew," he began, "had his whole family murdered by the Germans. One morning, I think it was a few days after the end of the occupation, he was staring from a window on the second floor of his house. He saw a German soldier running down the middle of the street. He ran down the stairs and out the door. The soldier was a few feet ahead, and the professor flung himself at him, catching his legs. The surprised soldier fell heavily to the pavement, knocking his head against a cobblestone. The professor looked up and saw an abandoned butcher shop, its windows smashed, its door gone. He carried the German into the shop and hung him by his neck from a meat hook, a very large hook intended for the carcass of a cow."

I stared at him, holding my breath. He embraced me suddenly and said, "I hope you have an easy trip to Warsaw."

I looked after him, but he didn't turn as he made his way through the station.

As I walked up the steps and into the interior of the car, carrying my small suitcase, I thought about the smile that had not left his lips from the time I had met him at the airport and during his recounting of the stories I had just heard.

I had thought it was a grimace of pain and embittered amusement, more or less permanent. But as I settled onto a wooden seat, it came to me that it was a further punishment for the crimes that had been committed against him, that he should always be caught midway between raging laughter and lamentation.

AFTER THE SNOW

I arrived in Warsaw at midnight after an arduous train journey from Prague. In their retreat, the Germans had nearly destroyed Poland's railroad system, and our train with its few passengers took four times as long to reach Warsaw as it had before the war.

The train halted for hours in vast frozen tracts. Inside the cars, the glacial air kept us motionless on hard wooden benches in a silence broken only by the faint whisper of our shallow breathing. Sometimes we halted in villages so small they barely disturbed the surface of the snow. At these stops, seemingly purposeless, some of us stood on the ice-coated train steps and leaned out as any traveler might, looking for a sign of life. Once three women emerged from several hovels clustered near the track, kerchiefs binding their heads, and ran heavily toward us, holding up mugs of steaming tea and pressing them into our frozen hands.

There were moments when I thought we might never feel again those grinding lurches forward that had marked the hours since we left the Prague station. I began to imagine that we would simply fade away, to remain only a memory to some peasant who had once seen our train moving sluggishly through that forsaken landscape.

But we did arrive at last at the temporary Warsaw railroad station. Behind it, in almost total darkness, a few droshkies waited. Horses snorted and stamped their hooves, and the drivers were huge and shapeless in their greatcoats and scarf-wrapped faces. In one of those small carriages, I rode into the silent city. Here and there, like the flow of banked fires, light shone from out of mountains of rubble and revealed the black ruins snow had not covered.

We entered the walled courtyard of the hotel Sir Andrew had spoken about. A guard wearing straw boots and carrying a rifle stepped out of the shadow of a portico, spoke a few words to the driver as I paid for the ride with zlotys I had bought in Prague, and watched me closely as I walked into the narrow lobby. There was no one there.

Carrying my one suitcase, I walked down a long corridor. I could smell fresh plaster. Suddenly I heard the opening measures of a Chopin étude. The source of the music was a small loudspeaker attached to the ceiling above the threshold of an immense dining room. I found out later that the hotel had been constructed with miraculous speed to accommodate ministers of the soon-to-be-elected Polish government, the first since the end of the war. The dining room too smelled of plaster and paint, but still it suggested a kind of faded splendor like that of the salons of grand hotels I had seen in other European cities.

As I stood there, bewildered by the brilliance of the lights, staring at the white columns that supported the high ceiling, I realized I was not alone.

Leaning against a circular food bar in the center of the room was a Polish officer, one black-booted foot in front of the other as though he might leave in an instant. He heard me put down my suitcase, turned toward me indolently, nodded, and went on eating a hard-boiled egg he held in the fingers of one long pale hand. No waiter appeared. We remained alone, the officer, the music, me. I had the sensation of being in a dream that belonged to someone else. Later, a clerk found me half asleep at a table and led me to a room, where I fell into bed with my clothes on.

The next morning I moved to a cheaper hotel, the Centralny, where I stayed until the middle of February, 1947, among other less affluent members of the press corps.

Most of the people who came to Warsaw that winter were journalists sent to observe and report on the election. There were other foreigners—relief experts, economists, architects, embassy personnel, and the various technicians who follow upon disasters. The journalists represented all shades of political opinion, and they wrote their stories for every kind of publication, from *The Times* of London to midwestern agricultural quarterlies. There were stars among them, like Dorothy Thompson and Ralph Ingersoll. Some were stringers like me with tenuous ties to wire services in Paris or London or New

York. But there were a notable few whose presence remained mysterious and who, apparently, represented only themselves.

Such was an Indian from Kashmir, frequently observed hurrying through the ravaged streets, his coat flapping open in that terrible cold, looking for bridge partners for himself and his friend, an elderly Polish countess who lived in the cellar of a bombed pastry shop. Another was a very young Englishman always wrapped in a shabby black ulster, who waited patiently and shamelessly for invitations to meals and was rumored to be a spy, a morphine addict, and not English at all, in fact, but a member of a Hungarian fascist youth group, and who, it was said by some, was stark naked under his coat. There was the Irishman from Limerick who strode through the rubble and snow in shabby riding boots, smacking one gauntleted hand with the quirt he always carried in the other, and who had distinguished himself by remarking that the wreck of the old Warsaw railroad station was the most aesthetically satisfying bomb site in all of Europe and England.

The cold was so intense that like many others I took to wearing sheets of newspaper under my coat. There was hardly any public transportation, a few streetcars to whose sides people clung like flies on a lump of sugar, two or three buses, a few tiny cars with no windshield wipers and perpetually fogged windows, and some motorbikes with wooden seats strapped on the front, from which, after the shortest ride, one toppled like a stone.

Most of us walked or, when we could afford it, hired a droshky. In its chilled depths, weighed down by mangy foul-smelling bearskin rugs, one fell into a snowbound trance as the droshky, drawn by a horse whose head hung disembodied amid the vapor of its own breath, made its way down a street or across the bridge over the frozen Vistula River.

Late at night, Warsaw was dark, except for an infrequent kerosene lamp glimmering from the debris where a room or less-defined space had remained intact. The wind that blew through the city came all the way from Lake Ladoga far to the north, and it was often so fierce that I wondered why it didn't dislodge the fire escapes and bathtubs hanging from the shells of the blasted buildings.

On nights when there was a moon, its light shone through the holes of windowless ruins that surrounded the heart of the city like a black frieze. To walk in Warsaw as I often did in the late evening, my chin buried deep in my collar, snow and debris piled up on every side, was to feel the cold and desolation and silence of a city of the dead. When the thaw came, we were told, the corpses of those who had fallen in the Warsaw uprising would be exposed.

During the day the streets were crowded, ringing with the noise of the living. Women sold giant cans of UNRRA fruit juice displayed on crudely carpentered shelves. Men peddled fountain pens, razor blades, whatever they could carry in their pockets. Loudspeakers in the city center broadcast Chopin all day long, and the crystals of snow glittered in the pale sunlight of snowless days and seemed to echo and reflect the notes of music.

The Centralny was a two-minute walk from the comfortable well-lit Hotel Polonia, with its spacious restaurant, where you could order what was said to be the best schnitzel in Warsaw.

To have a kind friend at the Polonia meant you could take a weekly bath there, and not have to ask one of the Centralny's two servant girls to carry bucket after bucket of hot water up its narrow staircase—the elevator never worked—to the hotel's only tub, which was in a bathroom on the third floor. On the second was a small café, where one could get scrambled eggs and vodka, real Moscow vodka in little pale-blue bottles.

Cigarette smoke, strong drink, and conversation in a dozen languages sent you off to your narrow room with an illusion of warmth that lasted until you slid between sheets that were like frozen lead. Scandals, private or political, gave a hectic animation, a spurious intimacy to exchanges between people who had nothing in common except proximity. The election was a foregone conclusion. The would-be suicide at the Bristol Hotel, where mostly the British stayed, had tried the same trick in Paris six months earlier over a different man. The Communist secret police had dossiers on every journalist in Warsaw. A Reuters man was having an affair with a short stout Bulgarian woman, despite the fact that the Bulgarian delegation kept her locked up at night in her hotel room in the Polonia.

No one spoke about the Jews, not in public. But in private there was much speculation about how many were still living in Warsaw. Some said a dozen. Others guessed several hundreds. They were hidden, like the Russian soldiers in their garrison on the other side of the Vistula, out of sight of the Poles.

When I think of the Jews of Warsaw, it is not the ghetto that comes first to my mind but Mrs. Helen Grassner, who arrived by plane a few days before the election. She had a room at the

Polonia. We became acquainted right after she was attacked by a boy who sold newspapers outside the hotel entrance.

No one knew his name or where he came from. He lived, as many other people did that winter, in some hole in the ruins. It was rumored that he was around fourteen. He looked ancient, timeless. A wooden peg was attached to the stump of his right knee. Although he could only hobble, he crossed the ground like a rat, muttering to himself all the while and from time to time emitting a terrifying cackle.

It was early evening when Mrs. Grassner stepped down from the droshky that had brought her from the airport to the Polonia entrance. I stood a few yards away, about to join a friend for tea in the dining room. The boy swung an armful of inky newspapers up at Mrs. Grassner's face, shouting in Polish—I knew he was demanding she buy one—and when she attempted to pass him, he cracked her across the shin with his peg, balancing himself on the crooked stick he carried and accompanying the assault with his deranged shriek.

She cried out, dropped her purse on the snow, and covered her face with her hands. I grabbed her elbow, retrieved the purse, and pulled her into the lobby. She looked at me with one hand against her cheek and bent her head to look at her leg.

"My God! What was that?"

"He does it to everybody," I said quickly.

"Everybody?" she said, in a dazed voice.

"If they don't buy a paper. The best thing is to give him a wide berth. He doesn't see so well."

"A savage!" she exclaimed.

"He just doesn't give a damn for anything," I said.

"I'm not surprised," she said. "I'm not surprised at all."

I was still holding her arm. She glanced at my hand, thanked me, and said she'd best go to her room and put something on the bump. "I can feel it swelling," she said.

After that I saw her everywhere, at the Foreign Ministry for press handouts, at hotel press conferences given by politicians, even in the offices of architects who were working on plans for the reconstruction of Warsaw. There was no special uniformity of dress among reporters, but Mrs. Grassner, in her dark neat suit and plain white blouse, always seemed out of place among us. She wore rubber overshoes, and her tight gray curls were flattened beneath a small felt hat. Her muskrat coat fell to mid-calf. Occasionally I would see her write something down in a notebook. More often she sat or stood on the outskirts of the crowd of reporters like someone waiting for a telephone call.

She looked like, and was, a suburban housewife. Her credentials, I discovered, were from a Jewish women's organization in the Midwest. The organization had sent her to Poland to see what the government intended to do for Jews who wanted to leave Poland and settle in what was then British-governed Palestine.

She spoke to me without a formal greeting, picking up our conversation from the day before about the weather. She suffered intensely from the cold and spoke of it bitterly. On election day, just before I left with a group of reporters for Radom in a car provided by the authorities, ostensibly to observe the voting, I found Mrs. Grassner in the Polonia dining room, drinking tea.

"Aren't you going to any of the polling places?" I asked her.

"Why should I?" she replied, and blew her nose. "What's to see? You think there'll be a surprise or something?"

"Well, just for interest."

"I'm not interested," she said.

Irritated, I left and went out to the car. How had she managed to get anyone to send her to Poland? Why didn't she buy proper boots?

The election passed. From a balcony in the new Parliament House, we watched Boleslaw Bierut being driven slowly in an open Mercedes through a double file of Polish cavalrymen as snow fell in large soft flakes. Later that day the new president held a press conference in the Winter Palace (or perhaps it was the Summer Palace—I've forgotten). Then there was a party.

I turned toward the windows of the great reception hall, away from the long tables laden with vodka and Tokay wine, caviar, and Polish ham. I could see through the dusk the snow-drenched woods where Polish royalty had once kept herds of deer. Mrs. Grassner had not come to the party, although even the Limerick Irishman was there, gobbling up caviar.

I didn't see Mrs. Grassner until a few days later when, with twenty or so other reporters, I waited in front of the Polonia for the bus that was to take us on a ten-day tour of Silesia. Mrs. Grassner stepped from the entrance, cast a quick glance up and down the street to make sure the newsboy wasn't there— he never was in the morning—and walked over to me. She nodded.

"I hope the bus is heated," she said.

"Oh, it will be," I assured her.

"Nothing is guaranteed," she observed.

It was a small bus with hard seats. Along with Mrs. Grassner and me, there was one other American, a young man, whose knowing smile, with its peculiar note of triumph, was always there when I glanced in his direction. It was as if everything that happened in Poland was in accord with some agreeable program of his own. Also among the party was an English-woman, three Czechs, and three Yugoslavs. Ottokar, the oldest Czech, was everyone's favorite, even the Polish officials at the Foreign Ministry. He looked older than his age, forty, and his gaze held such simple kindness that in response to it, I had noticed, people smiled gratefully.

After dinner in the village where we spent our first night away from Warsaw, the Czechs grew merry. The two younger men danced; they were quick and inventive with the controlled bright force of acrobats. Ottokar sang.

Before the Nazi invasion of Czechoslovakia, Ottokar had been a concert singer. Now he was a political columnist for a Prague journal. The Nazis had put him in a concentration camp in Breslau—Wroclaw in Polish—where he had spent three of his four years in solitary confinement. The other Czechs had been in camps too, Karel for four years and the one we all called Baby for two. The Yugoslavs had been partisans under Tito's command. These six men became the heart of our group, the center of nearly everyone's attention, as though their presences were a continuing drama of endurance and survival enacted now against a backdrop of snow-blanketed fields, raw new factories, and the ancient villages our little bus took us through.

Ottokar's last song that night was a wordless lament which, he told us, was sung by border guards along the Hungarian frontier. His voice broke in the middle of it. He became silent. Then the Englishwoman, Mary, stout and very young, sung to us in her sweet soprano about the Molly Maguires, massacres and betrayals, and Irish boys with bullets in their breasts, fallen on the moors.

During all of this, Mrs. Grassner sat alone in the small dining room of the provincial hotel where we were to spend the night. She neither smoked nor drank, nor did she applaud the singing as the rest of us did. When I passed by her table on my way to bed, I saw she had made a dozen or more neat piles of bread crumbs.

She did not go with us to the wagon-wheel factories, the day nurseries for working mothers, the mines, the new municipal buildings, or the evening parties. At first I thought her absence might be explained as a result of her dislike of the cold, that and a fundamental dullness of outlook. But then, at some point, perhaps in a hotel lobby in Katowice, she started to talk to me about something other than the weather.

"English and my poor Yiddish won't do," she began softly, more to my ear than to me. "I wish I'd learned better."

I reminded her that we were often provided with interpreters as we traveled about. "Oh, yes!" she exclaimed with a touch of bitterness. "That's all right for all of you! But I have different fish to fry. Where I have to go I need at least German."

"The Czechs speak German," I said.

She gazed broodingly at the floor. "That young one, Karel," she began. "You know he was four years in a camp?" I nodded, surprised she had learned that much.

"I know a lot of Jewish people and every one of them has lost relatives, whole families. But I didn't. How could that be? It's hard to believe that my whole family got away. I keep thinking: There must have been a cousin, even a distant cousin, murdered by them, the Nazis. But no. I have been informed there was no such cousin."

She spoke in an expressionless voice but her face, as though animated by feelings her tone concealed, began to crumple until, at last, tears ran down her cheeks. She opened her purse and skinned out a handkerchief with one small delicate finger, wrapped it around her nose, and blew.

"Don't think I'm not grateful," she said. "But I feel like a ghost. I've had such troubles . . . operations, disappointments, sadness . . . and now I'm a ghost."

Her purse slid off her lap. I picked it up and handed it to her. She seemed unaware of taking it. She stared at me intently, then shook her head from side to side. "Well, how would you know, a young girl like you?"

Late that evening, as we idled at the tables in the restaurant where we'd eaten dinner, a drunken soldier burst through the curtain that hung over the door. He peered at us with bleary blue eyes. His jacket was torn and his blond hair rose in spikes. He had a vehemently Polish face, a turned-up nose, and cheeks reddened by cold and alcohol. As he staggered between our tables, he appeared to have sprung from the pages of a Polish fairy tale.

The Yugoslavs toasted him and gave him a drink from their private store of slivovitz. He stood still an instant to drink. He was disheveled, laughing, nearly incoherent, and his mood veered as suddenly as he did. He whispered hoarsely to the glass

as though blaming it for being empty, held it out for more, frowned, and seemed to age before our eyes. Ottokar rose swiftly from his chair, put his arm around the soldier, and tried to lead him out of the restaurant. But he became stubborn and stamped the floor with his boot. Mrs. Grassner got to her feet, looking stricken. She left the room hastily, casting one horrified glance at the drunken Pole.

Later Karel, in his rudimentary French, asked me why Mrs. Grassner had left so abruptly.

"The soldier frightened her, I think," I replied.

"She's a Jew, isn't she?" he asked.

"Yes."

"She lost her family in Poland?"

"No."

"In another place?"

"She told me she lost no one."

"But she feels it all the same," he said. "When they have no dead, people feel it worse, somehow." I couldn't tell from his tone whether he was asking a question or giving an answer.

When we departed the next morning, Karel asked me to find out if Mrs. Grassner would share his bus seat with him. When I passed on his request to her, she looked surprised and then shrugged. "As long as it's not one of those Yugoslav lummoxes," she said.

She and Karel sat silently together during the morning. At some point, perhaps when we stopped for lunch, they must have discovered a middle ground between her Yiddish and his German, because in the afternoon they were talking together animatedly. From where I sat, just behind them, I could see that she was smiling.

In Wroclaw, we were given a day free of tours. Ottokar walked up to me in the hotel lobby and asked if I'd take a short trip with him. He didn't say where we were going.

We rode a streetcar to the central square, where the town hall rose in monumental grimness toward low-hanging gray clouds. Snow flurries came and went. It was raw. Ottokar stared at streets that led off the square, now one, now another.

"I'm not sure," he said.

"Where are we going?" I asked.

"I was driven in a car with drawn shades. But I knew we were next to the river," he said.

It took another hour to find it, an ancient prison behind which barbed wire drew a vast rectangle around stone block-houses laid out like tombs. The wind from the Oder River whipped us as we stood on a narrow street between the water and the prison. There was no one within sight.

"One winter," he began, "they let me out to toss garbage in the river. They let me do it for a week. It was heaven to be out-doors, to hear human voices, to see the moving water." He suddenly clasped me around my shoulders. "After all, it was only a dream," he said. "What else could it have been?"

We walked back to the square. By then the snow was falling heavily. I looked at Ottokar's face now and then. He was aware of my glances. I felt he knew what was in my mind, knew, as I suddenly did, that there was nothing more he could tell me.

Arrangements had been made for us to attend the opening of the opera house that night, the first time a concert had been

given there since the beginning of the war. Our Wroclaw interpreter told us to dress warmly. "There are holes in the roof from
the bombing," he said.

Even after the musicians had taken their seats, even when
the audience filled the loges and orchestra, that penumbral cav-
ern with its smell of dust and damp felt like a catacomb. There
was something wrong with the electricity, and the lights
couldn't be dimmed without plunging us into total darkness.
Only the Brahms violin concerto was played. The violin soloist,
a short dumpy woman wearing a short black dress, resembled
Mrs. Grassner. She wore mitts; I could see from the box where I
was sitting that they were woolen gloves with the fingers cut
off. The musicians wore ordinary suits. Some were without
neckties.

We all listened so intently that it was as though we had
never heard music nor would again. The Yugoslavs leaned forward, resting their chins on the worn velvet backs of the empty
seats in front of them. At the end, the audience gave the per-
formers a standing ovation, but the soloist and the musicians
hurried offstage to their coats and hats before the applause died
down.

As we walked back to the hotel, Karel asked me where Mrs.
Grassner had been. I said I didn't know.

"The violinist was a Jew," he said.

Mrs. Grassner was sitting in the lobby when we arrived at
the hotel. She motioned me to a nearby chair.

"You should have come to the concert," I said, as I sat down.
"The soloist was Jewish."

"I know, I know," she said, with a certain impatience. "She's a public figure, a well-known artist. I'm not thinking about her. It's the others."

"The others?" I repeated.

"My contacts. Don't you know *anything*? They don't let the Jews leave this country. Oh, yes, they promise transportation. Everything. They even make nice broadcasts to Palestine."

"Have you been seeing your contacts every place?"

"Every place, when I can find them," she replied.

I had been so sure she was huddling in blankets, alone in her hotel room, while we had been herded through factories, that even now I couldn't visualize her hurrying down streets to meet with fellow Jews. Didn't I know, she was asking, that the Poles were the worst anti-Semites in Europe? Had I imagined that Hitler had instructed *them* how to kill Jews? I had better think again, she said.

"That soldier! Did you look at his face? The drunken bum. When he came to the restaurant, I felt he was there to murder me!"

At that moment I recalled a young translator from the Foreign Ministry who had told me, as we stood talking on a street corner, shielding our faces with our hands against the glacial wind, that years before the war, on that very corner, he and other boys had chased Jewish children with razor blades tied to sticks.

Our last stop was a village near Swidnica, where we were to spend the night. It was only a few miles from the Czech border, so Karel and Baby were to leave the tour there and return to Prague. Their reportorial assignments were finished; they had no further reason to stay on. We were all cheered by our village accommodations, a comfortable old farmhouse with a large stove in the central hall whose heat rose up through a wide stairwell to warm the two floors where our bedrooms were.

I was to share a room with Mary, the Englishwoman, and a Frenchwoman, Mademoiselle Tetreault, a dour middle-aged person who was writing a series of articles on Polish working women for a French weekly. Until that night, I had hardly spoken to her. As Mary and I were emptying our suitcases, she observed that Mrs. Grassner had managed to get a small room for herself. She spoke French as though certain Mary and I would understand. As it happened, we did, but the assumption riled Mary who remarked, coldly, in French, "How can that possibly matter?"

"I would like to know, simply, how she managed to ensure her privacy. After all, I might have enjoyed a room to myself," Mlle. Tetreault responded.

"Then do ask Mrs. Grassner to exchange with you," Mary said.

"I am not in charge of arrangements," Mlle. Tetreault said.

The village was of particular interest. I had heard in Warsaw that the population was entirely Jewish. The government, it was said, had resettled the village with Jews who had found refuge during the German occupation in the Soviet Union. The next day we were taken by our guide to a shop where several tailors sat cross-legged on long tables as they worked. When they heard Mrs. Grassner speaking Yiddish to them, they looked up from their work at her, their faces eager and surprised and touched with some emotion I couldn't name.

The mayor of the village, a short stocky man who snapped

his fingers while talking to us through the interpreter and laughed often, led us down a narrow lane toward the market square. The only color on the ground was the snow-dusted piles of frozen horse manure. The mayor had spent years in prison before escaping to the Ukraine, the interpreter said, his voice muffled by a huge woolen scarf.

"One of those tough Jews," remarked the young American journalist. Mrs. Grassner gave him a suspicious look. She quickened her pace until she was walking beside the mayor. She said a few words to him in Yiddish. He took her arm vigorously in his own and then motioned us to halt.

On the side of the path was a sign nailed to a post in German. The mayor pointed to it, spoke rapidly to Mrs. Grassner, snapping his fingers, and laughed. Mrs. Grassner turned to us. "That's a sign the Nazis put up," she explained. "It says no Jews will ever walk this way again."

The mayor clapped his hands. Mrs. Grassner smiled broadly at him. She told me later that it was not the Germans but the Poles who had put the mayor in prison. "He was a radical," she said.

During the afternoon we were taken to a farm a few miles from the mayor's village. "It's a Jewish farm," Mrs. Grassner told me. There was no remarkable change in her voice. Her inappropriate lady's hat was clamped on her head in its usual position. Yet she radiated a peculiar energy, like the heat thrown off by a fever.

In the farm kitchen we were given large jugs of fresh milk to sample. The pale young farmer pointed proudly at a new stove, then led us through a covered passage to his barn. Once there, he grabbed up handfuls of grain from a sack and let it run through

his fingers, smiling shyly as he did so. When we returned to the
kitchen, the farmer told us what the government was doing for
him. His wife joined us, carrying a tiny infant, as pale as his
father, with the same round, colorless cheeks. It did not seem
possible that the three, so small and frail, could survive the hard
winter.

When we returned to our farmhouse, Mrs. Grassner said,
"That was supposed to be a surprise visit. But it was arranged.
The farmer told me in confidence that the authorities *always*
bring foreigners to his farm. It's the only good one, he says.
Besides, there are very few other Jewish farms. Don't you be
fooled!" Her voice was uncharacteristically fierce. "In this country, these people only want Jews to keep selling each other
shoelaces. You see?"

We had a good dinner and a lively evening. Ottokar and
Mary sang for us until their voices grew hoarse. Warmed by
vodka, we all decided to take a late walk. Mary and I wandered
off, listening to the Yugoslavs singing in the next narrow
street. Their voices grew fainter. At last the silence was broken
only by the snorting of horses in the nearby stables or the thud
of their hooves as they shifted their weight. It began to snow.
The street we were following ended abruptly at the edge of a
large open field that appeared to be hanging like a sheet from
the sky, tied to it by dark threadlike branches of pine trees.

Back in the farmhouse, Mary and I stood next to the stove,
warming our hands. Above us came the murmur of voices as
people got ready for bed. The outer walls of the house were as
thick as a fortress but the inner walls, put up to subdivide the old
rooms, were thin as straw. Upstairs, we found Mlle. Tetreault in a

long-sleeved salmon-colored nightgown sitting on the edge of her bed examining her fingernails.

"Nail polish cracks in this weather," she remarked.

Later, as I returned from the bathroom in the hall, I could hear voices rising clearly from the stairwell. I glanced down and saw Karel and Mrs. Grassner sitting side by side in front of the stove, their feet resting on an encircling iron rim.

Suddenly I felt uneasy. Mrs. Grassner, whom I had had the presumption to regard with a certain unthinking tolerance, had escaped my definition of her. She was as large as life.

I went back to the room, where I found Mary playing solitaire with a worn pack of cards and Mlle. Tetreault filing her fingernails. A few minutes later, we heard Mrs. Grassner's door open and close. Karel's voice, although it was only a whisper, came to us clearly. Mlle. Tetreault lifted her head as we heard the sound of kisses.

"*Sans pudeur,*" muttered Mlle. Tetreault.

"Hush!" hissed Mary.

"Don't address me in such a way!" Mlle. Tetreault protested. She rose to her feet, her throat taut, her mouth drawn down, and snatched a hairbrush from her toilet bag. "People are too irresponsible," she said, as she began to brush her hair violently.

Mary unpacked and repacked her suitcase and went back to her solitaire. I sat on a bench beneath a high window against which snowflakes clicked. Mlle. Tetreault punished her hair. Imprisoned by the muffled sounds from the room next door, we made our futile gestures. I picked up a Polish newspaper from the floor and stared at it, the ink staining my damp hands.

"Oh, well," Mary murmured, goodwill struggling with some

other emotion in her face. She beckoned me to her bed. Aimlessly, she dealt out cards and we played rummy. Mlle. Tetreault put down her hairbrush at last.

"I'm going to sleep," she announced loudly.

"Aren't you cold?" Mary asked me. I nodded yes. We heard Mrs. Grassner's door open and close. He had left. Mary and I threw down our cards.

"An old woman like that!" exclaimed Mlle. Tetreault. "How could he!"

"She's no older than you are," whispered Mary. "And keep your voice down."

"Ugly," Mlle. Tetreault said, but in a lower voice.

"He's sorry for her," Mary said to me. "You saw that? Listening to her in that nice respectful way of his? Keeping the wind from her in the square this morning? Did you notice? It's their business, anyhow."

I thought of how Mrs. Grassner had talked about her troubles with impatience and contempt, as though she'd been cheated of what was important by things that didn't count.

"It's because he isn't a Jew," I said, "but went through those years in the camp."

"I saw the tattoo on his wrist, the numbers, when he reached for a piece of bread at table," Mary said. "It was blue and blurred, but you could see what it was." She smiled absently. "Ah, well," she added, "our tour wouldn't have been complete, would it, without a little romance?"

The tension, along with the last vestiges of warmth, had left the room. I crept into bed. I felt an obscure gratitude toward Mary but I was too sleepy to think about it.

The next morning, Mrs. Grassner and Karel took the back two seats in the bus. Mlle. Tetreault didn't look at them but Mary and I turned around more often than was tactful. I don't know what I expected to see. Mrs. Grassner's head was bowed and, although they weren't talking, Karel bent toward her as though listening.

An hour or so later, the bus stopped at a fork in the road where Karel and Baby were to leave the tour and return to their own country. They shook hands with each of us, embraced Ottokar, and went down the two steps and out the bus door. Mrs. Grassner followed.

I wiped my window clear of vapor and saw Baby walk away from Mrs. Grassner and Karel, who were standing close to each other. She shivered. The snow was driven by wind gusts so intense as to rock the bus. Karel took off his glove and held out his hand to her. She took it in her own. Suddenly she brought his hand to her cheek, then let it drop.

When she got back on the bus, Ottokar took the seat next to her and put his arm across her shoulders. Karel and Baby were no longer visible through the window. I could see their tracks filling up with new snow.

Soon after our return to Warsaw, I began my preparations to leave. I needed an exit visa and a seat on a flight to Paris. On my last day, I walked about the city until I ached with cold. I went to the Warsaw ghetto again to stare at that great emptiness, but this time I went by bus. As it happened, just as we reached its perimeter, the bus was stopped by a bomb rolling in front of it, perhaps dislodged by a shifting ruin. We sat for an hour, waiting for the bomb squad to disarm it.

When I returned to the Centralny, I found a message. Mrs. Grassner would like to see me in her room at the Polonia. I drank a cup of hot tea, hurried over, and was about to walk through the hotel entrance when the newspaper boy screeched like a night bird and hobbled toward me with his armload of newspapers. I leaped out of his way and into the lobby.

I found Mrs. Grassner sitting on her bed, wearing her hat and overshoes.

"I hear you're leaving," she began.

"Yes." She looked at me somberly. "I'm going to Spain," I added.

"Spain," she echoed. "Well, I wanted to show you something before you left." She pointed at a large bolt of dark wool cloth on the bed. It was similar to the material of her suit. "I found a wonderful place for wool," she said. "You might like to go there."

"I haven't any money left," I said. "Just enough to leave."

"Oh," she said, as she stroked the wool lightly. "I still have a bruise on my leg from that devil at the door." She sighed then. "I'm leaving soon too. This cold . . . my nose began to run the day I arrived. I'm nearly out of handkerchiefs. I wonder if it ever warms up here."

"I heard that the snow can thaw as early as March," I said.

"And after that? What's there to see then?"

I didn't know how to answer her. Instead of trying, I asked, "Did you find out any more about all those things you were telling me on our bus tour?"

She bent over to unbutton her overshoes.

"I found out everything," she answered. She looked up at

me. For a second I thought I saw a flash of amusement on her face. Perhaps I only imagined it.

"So what do you think of my material?" she asked.

I tried, but I could think of nothing to say about the wool except that it looked as though it would wear well.

THIS ALL HAPPENED LONG AGO, AND IN A DIFFERENT WORLD. Helen Grassner would be dead now. The Czech, Karel, who looked like a boy, is old. If he is still alive.

MARIE

Among the Communists I knew in Los Angeles in 1940, most, I gradually came to think, were puritans who interpreted events in their lives, and daily life itself, according to an implacable system of thought that made them as insensible to the complexities of life as the petits bourgeois who fill the novels of Sinclair Lewis.

I was seventeen. I had no family to rebel against. I doubted that the day would arrive when the people on earth would share its wealth equally. The heroic virtues of the working class, to which I then belonged, eluded me. I was searching for shelter and community. If there was a comprehensible reason why I was attracted to the Communists, it was the racial justice they preached, that and their certainties about life, which comforted me just as Sunday school had years earlier. There are no questions in heaven.

In Warsaw, when I was twenty-three, I came upon Marie, who was indirectly responsible for clearing away any vestiges of belief I may have had about the rule of the proletariat.

My room was narrow and sparsely furnished, with a cot, a folding chair, a roughly carpentered armoire, and a small basin stained by a not-quite-audible trickle of cold water from its single tap. My medium-sized suitcase stood on the floor.

Just behind the cot was a window that looked out upon the wall of what might once have been a large residence or an institution. Its bricks glittered with frost; its shattered windows framed fragments of gray sky. There were many days when my window was curtained with thick falling snow, and I could see nothing from it. The floor of the room was swept twice a week, most of the time, by one of the two Centralny servants. The one I came to know was Marie.

She was in her late twenties, tall, broad-shouldered, a gaunt brunette. She might have been handsome but for her habitual beseeching expression. When she caught me looking curiously at her, her mouth would widen in an anxious, placatory smile that reflected the coolness of her closed-off spirit.

She was taller than I but gave the impression of being shorter. As soon as I opened my door to her knock, she bent her head and shoulders as though bowing as she asked my permission to clean the room.

She was the one who brought pail after pail of hot water from the kitchen to pour into the bathtub in a tiny room with a toilet at the end of the corridor. Only icy water issued from one of the two taps. The Centralny elevator had not worked since the Warsaw uprising.

When I imagined Marie toiling up the stairs to the third floor, hoisting the pail to her shoulder, and pouring the water into the rust-stained tub, I hesitated to ask for more than one bath a week and made do with the basin in my room.

Toward the end of January, the British news service I worked for gave me an assignment to interview Count Radziwill. I approached him as he left the Senate building one morning, and we made a lunch appointment at the Polonia Hotel restaurant.

At noon I left my room to take the short walk to the Polonia, what would have been in prewar Warsaw two or three cleared blocks. Now there was no sidewalk, only a path through high banks of hardened snow. Across from the hotel, the bomb-blasted remains of the Warsaw train station, a monstrous heap of jagged steel beams and spirals of twisted train tracks, were flung upward, ending abruptly their mad ascent toward the snow-laden sky.

I passed the newsboy with his rat's face, holding a sheaf of newspapers in his filthy clawlike hand.

The street was like the crossroads of a fair, a festive party the point of which had long been forgotten, and the music that flooded the freezing air reminded me of clarity and a romantic benevolence denied by the craters and ruins of all that lay about me.

Inside the Polonia, I was surrounded by sofas and chairs, carpeted floors, and uniformed staff. Life in a hotel lobby as it had once been.

I was early for my lunch date, so I walked up a flight of stairs to say goodbye to Larry C———, the Associated Press journalist. I was leaving Warsaw the next day.

He opened his door with his usual disbelieving smile, which he might have been unaware of; it said to all comers, Show me! Prove it! I bet!

I asked him where he'd been on election day. Since then I'd only glimpsed him during press conferences at the Ministry of Foreign Affairs.

"There was nothing to see," he replied. "No surprises."

"I know," I said, a touch defensively. "But in Radom, where I went, I saw an old man, maybe eighty, voting for the first time in his life."

"Yeah?" he asked sardonically. "I wonder who he voted for?"

I was embarrassed by the intensity with which I'd spoken. It was a flame from an old fire, my sense of the injustices of life. Once again I'd judged an action for its own sake with no thought to its outcome.

I may have sighed. He stared at me with unexpected sympathy and asked if I was returning to the good ol' USA. Not at once, I answered. I planned a trip to Spain to look up a relative. The sympathy drifted from his face. "Have a good time," he said.

I left his room and went to meet the Count. When I arrived at the entrance to the dining room, a small solidly built man with an air of importance smiled at me and walked the few feet between us to take my arm and escort me to the table he'd reserved—although I was going to pay for the meal.

I had no expense account, and to my dismay he ordered course after course. I ate only soup, as slowly as I could.

The Count told me there had been a Radziwill in the Polish Senate since the sixteenth century, and there would be one in the coming term. He had won the votes he required against the Communists because, he explained with aristocratic self-deprecation, the party wanted a representative from the old Poland.

As a concession to President Bierut, he had made the journey to his land in eastern Poland and partitioned it among the peasants. There, in a hovel, he had celebrated with them. With an ironic smile, he told me what they had toasted with the liquor he had brought: *Death to the Mongols!* He laughed outright at the comedy of it.

I asked him how he had managed during the German occupation. He told me he had spent several years in a concentration camp, from which he had once tried to escape. But he had been shot in the calf by a guard as he ran across the compound at one in the morning. Unlike other prisoners, he had had the benefit of anesthesia while a doctor dug the bullet out of his leg.

When he regained consciousness, his first words were: "Will I ever be able to ride again?" He smiled and nodded at me, probably assuming I knew he had been speaking about horses.

It was, on the whole, an agreeable time I spent with him, although the bill wasn't agreeable. When we left each other at the hotel entrance, he looked at me with courtly amusement. "I hope to see you again," he said. I knew he never would.

I returned to the Centralny. There was one more thing to do: put my remaining zlotys in an envelope for Marie. I found her leaning on her elbow on the small counter, behind which stood the desk clerk. She was whispering to him in a furtive manner as if conscious she was stealing time from her duties. After we'd greeted each other, I asked her for her last name.

Her face flashed with fear. In a nearly inaudible voice, cringing as though I was about to cane her, she spelled out the Polish letters. We were standing a few feet from the counter, and she glanced back at the clerk as though he might save her.

I was frightened by her response to my question and went in search of someone who might explain it. Later that same day I met an English-speaking reporter who had spent more months in Warsaw than I. He told me Marie had taken fright because she thought I had been displeased with her service and was going to report her to the secret police. It was always that with the Poles these days, he said.

I was stricken.

The left had sheltered me for a while. I had not taken its political aims seriously. I had taken nothing seriously except the apprehension that had hounded me for most of my life and whose servant, all unknowingly, I had been.

I saw Marie once more. I pressed an envelope into her hands with its flap unsealed so she could see the corner of a zloty. She smiled, a ghost of worry lingering about her face as she thanked me.

WHEN I LEFT WARSAW THE NEXT MORNING ON AN ARMY transport plane, I was reminded of the ship on which I had crossed the Atlantic nearly a year earlier and the narrow berths and hammocks most of us had slept in.

There were still bucket seats along the aisle on the airplane, which gave it the drastic pared-down look of a machine for war. But there was a woman steward, an incongruity in that plane, like a hostess at a tea party in a bunker.

As the plane took off, we passed close over a line of German prisoners of war, digging a trench that would become the foundation of a new airport terminal, the present one being a windowless shed.

The pilot dipped the right wing steeply as if with the intention of decapitating the prisoners. They ducked, terrified, their heads bent close to their shovels. The passengers, including me, laughed heartlessly.

A moment later, a picture of Marie came to mind: her helplessness as she imagined what the secret police might do to her. In my mind's eye, Boleslaw Bierut stood at the same great window in the palace I had stood at briefly, staring at snow falling on trees among which deer had once wandered for a king's pleasure. Was it now the workers' palace?

My knowledge of socialism, and its ferocious cousin communism, had been spotty, frivolous, without judgment or any sense of responsibility. For a moment I slumped in the metal bucket seat, overcome by regret and self-revulsion.

CHILDREN OF THE TATRAS

One of the places I visited during the bus trip I took with other journalists was a former vacation estate of a Prussian aristocrat in the Tatra Mountains on the Polish-Czechoslovak border. The Polish government had converted it into a kind of recovery residence for children who had been born in concentration camps or had spent part of their childhood in them. Their parents, without exception, had been murdered by the Nazis.

Our small group of reporters arrived one midafternoon after a lengthy bone-chilling ride through the winter-silent landscape. It was not yet dark. There were twelve or thirteen boys and girls and a small staff in a grand but bleak house. Its walls were bare, its floors stripped of rugs; a few rooms had linoleum on the floors. The house's vast windows were white with glare from the snow-covered mountains.

It was impossible to tell the ages of the children, they were so stunted. They were very glad to have visitors, and they clung to us, grasping our hands as they showed us their classroom; a former salon, now filled with narrow, neatly made cots; a library long emptied of books, its shelves containing a few toys and games; and the dining room, where we ate an early supper on a table covered with yellow oilcloth.

After supper, the Englishwoman, Mary, gave a concert for the children. They sat with rapt attention as she sang in a language they didn't understand, but they understood the music.

Only one Yugoslav and two Czech journalists spoke Polish; the rest of us depended on an interpreter. The children wanted to know everything. Where had we come from and why? Did we live in houses? What were they like? If we had children, where were they, with us so far away? Had we left them with relatives or strangers?

They did not speak of their own histories except in the most indirect fashion, and not always in words. They were painfully alert to any sudden movement and fell into abrupt silences in the midst of merriment, when they seemed to sink into troubled dreams that raced like camera lights across their faces; then they would suddenly burst out into hectic, even frantic laughter.

A boy whose name in English would have been Richard asked me to call him that through the interpreter. He didn't want his Polish name; he'd thrown it away. He said he wanted me to accompany him to one of the huge gardens I had noticed as we approached the mansion. I thought he was nine or so. I was told he was fourteen.

We went through the French doors of the dining room. It was nearly dark now, but there was a rose-colored light on some of the mountain slopes. He held my hand as we walked along a partly cleared path, snow-laden branches of shrubbery leaning toward us, the bare branches of winter-blackened trees above. It was a somber, frozen, lonely place, the gelid heart of winter. Then he ran a few feet ahead of me and, with his arms and legs, brushed the snow from what I mistook as a column that had once supported a mythological or heroic statue. It was a very large birdbath.

He smiled at me and pointed at the sky. He made flapping motions with his arms more and more slowly as the wings of the bird he was imitating closed around his body and it landed on the rim of the birdbath. He turned his head, then stretched it forward as though to drink. His hands fluttered once again; his arms made flying motions; the bird flew away.

I applauded. He danced in triumph and then, making little clucking sounds that may or may not have been Polish words, he shook the snow from a bush nearby and motioned for me to look closely at what he was doing as he put his hands together beneath his chin, then gradually widened them. I caught on and kicked some snow away from the ground. The earth looked like iron.

I bent and made my arm into a stalk growing from the ground. I opened my fingers to sniff the petals of an imaginary

flower. He let out a small shout of laughter and grabbed my hand and pressed it against his head. I think he meant that I had understood that he had been miming the coming of spring.

Before we left that evening, the children sang for us. Their faces were flushed with the pleasure of performing. At our departure, they crowded around the great entrance doors of the house, stunted little weeping figures. They stood quietly while we walked down the cleared path to our little bus. But as we drove away, we saw them waving vigorously, to wish us a safe journey.

PERLITA

My great-uncle, Antonio de Carvajal, lived in a flat in a very old converted mansion on one of the broad avenues of Barcelona called *ramblas*. In the spring of 1947, I stopped working for Sir Andrew and left Paris to visit him. I had $100 with which to support myself for the month I hoped to stay in Spain, pay I'd saved from my job as a news-service stringer in Eastern Europe. It didn't leave enough for traveling, but after nearly a year in postwar Europe I had become practiced in converting my few pounds into other currencies at the best rates of exchange.

This was offered by professional black marketeers as well as by people who had once been teachers, engineers, actors, and musicians, and others with now-useless vocations, who had been exploded out of their ordinary days by the war and were drifting through the cities of Europe, waiting on the edge of hopelessness for work permits that might enable them to resume some version of their former lives.

I remember the clothes they wore, garments of dispersion, dark threadbare jackets, pants often held up by string, their cold-reddened hands thrust into torn pockets as they stood for hours in all kinds of weather near banks and post offices where foreigners tended to gather.

As I boarded the train in Paris, I was too young and too dumb to worry about entering a fascist country; what I was apprehensive about were my meager funds. But two days after I arrived in Barcelona, I was put in touch with a man who gave me a good exchange rate of pesetas for pounds. (The bills had been printed in Leipzig, in Germany.) He was a Republican doctor who was not allowed to practice medicine by the Falange. He earned a living of sorts in the black market. During the week, he could be found in any one of several Barcelona cafés. On weekends he went to the mountains with dozens of vials of penicillin to serve as best he could the medical needs of those remaining Republican soldiers and their families who lived there in desperate conditions.

Tío Antonio was my grandmother Candelaria's only surviving brother. I had spent a few years of my childhood with her in the United States and Cuba. Her brother was the only person she still corresponded with. I yearned to meet a relative who was a real European.

Tío Antonio was in his early seventies. He was a handsome benevolent-looking man with blue eyes and the large head of a

Basque. Part of the northern branch of the family were Basques from Asturia.

The origin of the Basques is obscure. No connection has yet been found between their language and other European language groups. It is known that they antedate the ancient Iberian tribes of Spain and resisted the invasion of the Visigoths from the north with great stubbornness. That they were unable to resist entirely is proved by the prevalence of reddish- and fair-haired people in Spain's northern provinces.

Luisa, Tío Antonio's housekeeper and, sometime after the death of his wife, his companion, told me that he had once been redheaded. By the time I met him, he had a white tonsure like a monk's.

IT WAS A VERY COLD SPRING, FOLLOWING WHAT WAS SAID TO have been the coldest winter in Europe for twenty years. A brazier of coals burned beneath the table where we often sat. From a wood chest, Tío Antonio took out his most valued books to show me. Some had been written by his friend, the Spanish philosopher Ortega y Gasset. As a young man, Tío Antonio had met with Ortega on many an afternoon, to drink thick Spanish chocolate in a café on one of the *ramblas* and to talk about Spanish Catholicism, politics, and life.

Tío Antonio had a small elderly dog; he could only guess at her age. He had seen her from his window. She was standing, apparently frozen with fear, among the railroad tracks that ran behind his building. Having just recovered from a severe pneumonia, he was extremely feeble and could barely walk. But with Luisa's help, he descended the long staircase (there was a cage elevator that had not worked for years and was not working when I was there) and went out to the tracks where, after nearly an hour, he managed to coax the dog to come to him and then to carry her up to the flat. It was, he said, half a blessing that the trains ran so infrequently.

He named the dog Perlita, Little Pearl. She was a stiff-legged animal, white-furred except for a few mustard-colored patches. She had the look of a circus dog in an old engraving. She was not unfriendly but had an air of world weariness; she was a dog who had been through too much to be especially enthusiastic about anything in this life. But her gravity and oddly professional look were immensely appealing.

The cause of my great-uncle's frailty at the time when he rescued Perlita was political and bitter. Several months before he saw the little dog among the railroad tracks, he had written a letter to my grandmother on Long Island to thank her for some sacks of sugar she had sent him for Luisa to exchange on the black market for food. He had a pension of sorts, but it did not go far in those straitened days, and a few pesetas and supplemental food eased life a little. In the letter, he expressed his hope that since Europe had been liberated from the Nazis, Spain too might be liberated from General Francisco Franco and his Falange. A young cousin from Cadiz was visiting him at the time. The same day he finished and mailed it, she went to a police station half a mile away and reported to an official there that her elderly cousin had written a treasonable letter to his sister in America.

The political branch took Tío Antonio to the police station, held him for nearly a week in a cold damp cell without a blanket to cover himself or a board to lie down on, and beat him, although not as severely as they might have a few years earlier when the power of the Axis would have inspired their blows with greater savagery. Now and then they gave him something to eat. He was an old man and the insult to his body was great, but there is more to being beaten than the suffering of the flesh.

He was a retired doctor. He had been a colonel in the army. He, like his friend Ortega, had written essays on philosophy, on Spanish history, and against the clergy. He told me about Miguel Primo de Rivera, the Spanish general whose dictatorship was established the year I was born and whose only good deed, Tío Antonio said, was to order that the horses ridden by picadors in bullfights be blanketed around their bellies to spare them from evisceration in the arena. He spoke of the monarchy, of Carlists, of Alcalá Zamora y Torres and his efforts to distribute church property, of Anarcho-Syndicalist rebellions in Catalonia, of Manuel Azaña and the Popular Front, and of Franco, always in terms of character: ignobility of spirit, malice, ambition, and human blindness, as though politics were no more and no less than direct aspects of human temperament. I understood that much, although the array of names and events bewildered me.

Luisa went to the police station each day he was there, taking food and warm clothing that was not given to him. And she was there that cold dusk when he was thrust out the door to faint in the street.

He was ill for a long time. It was during his convalescence that he saw the little dog and saved her.

Perlita was such a strange creature. She would stand for a long time at the threshold of a room as though awaiting a sign. She was quite plump by the time I saw her. I asked him how he had fattened her up, for he had told me she was nothing but skin and bones when he rescued her.

"Sopa de ajo," he answered, smiling.

Garlic soup.

When I lived with my grandmother in a small suburban village on Long Island, she occasionally sent me off to school in the morning with a breakfast somewhat different from cereal and toast. She minced cloves of garlic and spread them on a slice of dark bread that had been soaked in olive oil. On those mornings, my arrival at P.S. 99 was greeted by my schoolmates with cries of mock horror and hands stretched out to warn me not to come any closer.

I was the foreigner in a school whose population was made up largely, as I recall, of working-class Irish Catholics. The final damning evidence of my foreignness was my grandmother herself, when she came to school on those days set aside for parents to visit the classrooms.

She did not in the least resemble any of the other parents. She was much older, of course. She had a thick Spanish accent. She looked like a Spanish woman from northern Spain.

I loved the dark bread covered with cloves of garlic and soaked in olive oil, and I did not give it up.

Prejudice has its own headaches. I was a puzzle to the other children. I was fair-haired and might have been taken for a Scandinavian. One branch of my family in southern Spain was descended from the Emirate of Granada. If the other children had known I had Arab ancestors from North Africa, they might have been entirely floored or chased me out of the school. As it was, they didn't know what to do with me. They settled for halfway measures, allowing themselves to torment me from time to time, becoming friendly when they forgot—as children will—what it was exactly they were tormenting me for. Toward the end of my time at the school, their attention was diverted from me by the arrival of two boys, also "foreigners," an Armenian and a French-Canadian whose accent was as heavy as my grandmother's. The three of us soon contrived a small country of our own.

When Tío Antonio told me what he had fed the starved Perlita, I recalled in one intense moment those puzzling, painful schooldays of mine. I looked at Perlita with a sense of comradeship. Garlic had saved her. In a way it had saved me too, confirming my position as an outsider and preventing me from absorbing easily any unquestioning assumptions of national superiority, so prevalent, so grotesque a phenomenon in our country, made up as it was and is, in large part, of transportees, captives, and immigrants.

When I think of Spain, I imagine my great-uncle sitting at the table, its wood warm from the heat of the coals in the brazier, Miguel de Unamuno's *The Tragic Sense of Life* open before him to the pages from which he is reading aloud to me, and Perlita standing quietly near him. After a while, she seems to feel it's safe to lie down, her back a few inches from the brazier, and a few minutes later she sleeps.

I see the great black stones of the police station. I did go look at it. A man emerged from the building as I stood there. He

was wearing a thin white raincoat, which I had learned all policemen wore who worked in the political branch. Fashions, I saw, existed also among fascist police.

He said something to me with a smile that meant he thought I was from Asturias. I felt a fleeting pleasure in that— not to be thought a foreigner. When I reluctantly shook my head, he asked me if I was English. I told him I was from the United States. He said, "I suppose you think we eat babies over here." I did, but I didn't say so.

I think of what is called *political life,* so abstract until a cane is laid across one's back. I think of the life of the spirit that would send a sick old man out to rescue a stray animal he had glimpsed on the railroad tracks. And I think of the civil wars, of the young cousin from Cadiz and her cruel act, licensed by ideology, and of the degradation and, finally, destruction of family and fellow feeling.

But what I see most vividly now, six decades later, is Perlita, saved!

As I look at her in my mind's eye, I am reminded not of the loftiness or dignity of the human spirit but, rather, its sudden capacity in dire circumstances for an overarching sympathy, its redemptive humbleness.

RETURN

On my last evening in Barcelona, I went in search of a place where I could hear flamenco music. I had met by agreement a friend of mine from California, Marjorie, and the young man from New York she was traveling with, Harold, who stayed in a hotel during the days I spent with Tío Antonio. The next morning the three of us were to travel by train to Madrid.

I wandered the streets of the city until, in a narrow dark alleyway, I heard the sounds of castanets clicking, heels hitting the floor, bursts of applause and then abrupt silence where the moment seemed to hold its breath, releasing it at last to the blazing intensity of guitar chords and the gravel-voiced singer who accompanied them with words of sorrow and carnality and death—the antithesis of the mild Christian church music I had heard during the early years of my childhood.

The audience heard the door open: its male members turned to stare at me, the dancers stopped, the guitar player paused with one hand in the air. My face turned red. I had seen at once that one of the dancers was naked from her waist to her black thick-heeled shoes. I retreated to the street, the fire in my face extinguished in the forgiving dark. The laughter of the men followed me until I reached a main avenue. I had opened the door to a whorehouse.

WE MET AT THE BARCELONA STATION THE NEXT MORNING and entered a third-class compartment. Seven or eight people had already taken their seats. Among them was a Guardia Civil, an old woman, and a man who turned out to be a doctor too, like the black marketeer with whom I had traded pounds for pesetas the second day I was in Barcelona.

The doctor on the train was also forbidden to practice medicine by the Franco regime. He scratched out a living as an assistant to a Madrid oculist. He had been sent to Barcelona on some business matter. Several passengers sat between him and the Guardia Civil, but the doctor looked over at him apprehensively. Then he whispered to me as the train crossed the Ebro River, "Here many brave men died in battle against *them.*"

I translated for Marjorie, while Harold tried to decipher a Barcelona newspaper he had bought at the station.

I had told the doctor that my mother was Spanish, and I was still fluent from my year on a Cuban plantation. But the doctor noted I had what he termed "an Antilles accent." He smiled sweetly as he said it.

It struck me all at once that I *was* half Spanish and took some pride in being so, even though I knew the poverty of such pride.

Tío Antonio had spoken of two distant female cousins of his who had lived in a run-down castle in Asturias. (They would have been cousins of mine too, though cousinhood tends to mean little as it becomes more remote.) On their estate, Mondragón, was a small chapel, and inscribed on the lintel were the words: TO THE SACRED MEMORY OF DON FELIX DEL CAMINO, INQUISITOR FOR NORTHERN SPAIN. There was a sixteenth-century date appended to it, presumably the year of his death.

By the end of the Spanish civil war, the two elderly women were widows. And a few months later both died within weeks of each other. I had forgotten to ask my great-uncle who owned the castle in 1946. Perhaps I was too surprised and amused by his story about the two sons, one for each widow. The first had grown up only to die early in the civil war, fighting for General Franco. The other had hemophilia and had been rejected as unfit by the Falangist army. But he had a profession.

The widows earned a small stipend from the government for showing the chapel and certain rooms in the castle to tourists who visited Asturia and had heard about Mondragón. The old sisters employed a part-time servant. Usually he was bare-footed, but when tourists were expected the servant put on shoes and white gloves and escorted the visitors into the chapel and then into the rooms in the castle.

One great salon, its walls covered with torn and faded scarlet silk, had no furniture except for a Ping-Pong table, with a paddle laid on either side of the net. The mother of the hemophiliac would then step forward and tell visitors that her son had been rejected by the army because of his ailment. But he *was* the Ping-Pong champion of Spain.

WE HAD BEEN TRAVELING FOR A FEW HOURS WHEN THE Guardia Civil took his canteen from a kit he carried. He began at once to eat his meal of potato omelet and bread.

A beggar woman immediately appeared at the door of the compartment and mutely held out her hand. The Guardia Civil tore off a small piece of bread and placed it in her lined, soiled palm.

"*¡Que richessa la da!*" exclaimed the old woman passenger, her words accompanied by an ironic smile. The Guardia Civil merely grunted and didn't look up from his canteen.

Several hours later, the train halted briefly at a station called Alcalá de Henares. Everyone in our compartment turned to me, even the Guardia Civil. Their faces were, for once, open and unguarded as the old woman said, "Here is the birthplace of Miguel de Cervantes Saavedra!"

AT THE MADRID STATION, A CONTINGENT OF SOLDIERS, WAIT-ing for a train perhaps, saw me and some of them called out, "*¡Andaluz!*" It was a joke. Andalusians tend toward shortness of body and darkness of hair; I was fair-haired and tall. But I found a certain comfort in their mockery—once again I was being taken for a Spaniard.

...

MARJORIE WAS A FREELANCE WRITER. WHILE WE WERE IN Madrid, she contacted a woman whose name she'd been given in New York City as someone who was in sympathy with the Republicans. Most of them—as the doctor on the train had informed me—lived in drifting communities in the mountains around Madrid. I thought the Falangistas probably knew of their existence—how could they not?—but they were willing to wait for them to die out rather than attack them. There were so pitifully few left. So many had strayed from their mountain strongholds hoping to be absorbed into the life of their villages and towns by way of shadow occupations, clerks, assistants of one kind or another, especially the professional people, among whom were doctors, teachers, and lawyers.

Marjorie and I visited the woman on our third and last day in Madrid. She lived in an apartment house not far from the Puerta del Sol, Madrid's city center. We rang the bell of her flat on the third floor. I heard her footsteps as she arrived at the door, then she hesitated before she let us in. Her expression was apprehensive.

She always feared the days on which the *Falangista policia* appeared at her door, she told us. They questioned her frequently. She suspected they knew about her contacts among the antifascists. Did they know, she wondered, that she met with the chief of the Madrid underground? They always came to her flat in the late afternoon, ringing her bell around the same time she was expecting her twelve-year-old daughter to come home from school.

I thought to myself what a state of dread she must feel every day as she waited to see whose thumb had pressed the bell, a child's or a policeman's, and the pained relief she must feel when she saw her daughter standing in her doorway.

We spent twenty minutes with her, asking questions about how she managed to live, how often she met with the chief of operations in the city, and how the mountain refugees fared, among whom was her husband, who had changed the name on his identity papers to protect her and their child.

We left her and went directly to the address she had given us of the Madrid underground chief so that Marjorie could interview him. He was an elderly man wearing spectacles that he took off every few seconds. He had moments of animation but mostly he seemed bewildered, and he gave out more personal information than he intended; a subtle emanation of defeat drifted around his puzzled being like motes of dust.

Harold, who showed little interest in political life, had gone to a museum. We met him later at a café, as arranged, and from there we went to the Madrid railroad station to take a train to Valencia. Harold and Marjorie were looking forward to seeing a bullfight, and I tried to control my shudders as they talked about it. When the train came, we separated, Marjorie and Harold to the second class car, where he had bought seats, and me to third class.

I sat down next to a large young woman who told me she was on her way to visit her husband, who had been interned in a prison village west of Valencia. I had not heard of prison villages until then. She told me that the prisoners had the run of the village but if they tried to leave, they were shot dead by the soldiers who were posted in a cordon around the outskirts.

Spanish Republicans, she said, often escaped over the Pyrenees to France, only to end up in bleak French internment camps, surrounded by barbed wire, for indefinite periods of time, waking each morning to empty days.

She told me of women who visited their husbands regularly in Spanish prisons to bring them food parcels. One day, a wife or a relative would arrive, only to be told their man would no longer need to eat anymore; he had "died from natural causes."

"Beaten to death," she explained, with a quick look around her at the other passengers.

The train halted at a small village and people scrambled and pushed inside through the open windows, grunting and groaning with the exertion, only to find there were no seats—the train was so crowded—so they sat on their bundles in the aisles. Soon after, the train stopped in the middle of nowhere and a detachment of Moorish soldiers boarded and stalked through our car. They seemed especially threatening, and my seat companion whispered to me that I must show my American passport somewhere, so I placed it on my lap. Two paused for a long minute, and one picked up the passport, examined it, and then, with a word I couldn't understand, dropped it back in my lap.

Once we arrived in Valencia, I rejoined Marjorie and Harold, and the three of us went to a hotel near the station.

THE NEXT DAY, THE TWO OF THEM WENT OFF TO THE BULL-fight. I went too but stopped at the entrance. They were flushed with excitement.

The street that circled the amphitheater was empty; the

brilliant sunlight picked out the imperfections in the exterior wall of the ring. I couldn't afford a ticket, but I wouldn't have bought one in any event. I was too frightened by what I would have to see.

I listened to the roars of the crowd, which rose and fell like ocean waves breaking; the military sound of the band and the assertions of the trumpet; and the groans and cries from the onlookers. When my friends emerged from the ring, I found it hard to speak to them for a while, even after Marjorie had said that it had been a horrible spectacle.

THAT EVENING, THE DAY'S MATADOR HELD A RECEPTION IN the salon of the hotel where we were to stay one more night before embarking on a small ship for the Balearic Islands.

Newspaper journalists who considered themselves aficionados of bullfights, and an entire entourage of hangers-on, were gathered about the star of the evening, no longer radiant, Marjorie noted, without his *traje de luces* but short and stocky and dull-looking in a business suit, unrecognizable to me except for his pigtail.

They noticed the three of us and, seeing we were foreigners, drew us into the animated circle they had made around the silent bullfighter, just as he had been encircled by the amphitheater earlier that day.

Beforehand, I had asked at the Prado museum to see Goya's black-and-white war drawings, and the young painter who was copying a Rubens work, with whom I was speaking, said the drawings had been removed to Toledo for an upcoming exhibition. In a Madrid bookstore, I requested a volume of Federico García Lorca's poetry. The clerk had blanched at the name but had gone to the back of the store and, after nearly fifteen minutes, had returned with a small volume of Lorca's work from which he was blowing the dust.

Now I asked one of the journalists, tall and elegantly dressed, if he had heard of a novel called *For Whom the Bell Tolls* by Ernest Hemingway. "But of course," he replied. "I reviewed it for my newspaper."

I was startled. My momentary flustering of the young painter in the Prado and the clerk in the bookstore had not worked with this journalist. But had Hemingway's novel been published in Spain?

He explained further. *Life* magazine had published pages of stills from the film that had been made, based on the novel. He had read the captions and written his review from them.

He smiled at me sympathetically. "Not much of a story," he said.

A BROWN RAIN FELL ON US THE NEXT MORNING AS, AMONG other passengers, we boarded a small ship that would stop at Ibiza, Majorca, and, after we had disembarked, Minorca. Harold planned to leave for Paris after two days. Then he would sail home to the United States.

My clothes were covered with damp brown spots so I inquired about the rain from a passing sailor. "A desert rain from North Africa, blown here by wind," he replied.

At twilight, the ship was heaving and pitching and rolling

from starboard to port and back, in a storm the wind had fore-told. Lights on shore exploded like fireworks. In the contained space of the Mediterranean, the storm felt much more violent than it would have if we hadn't seen the land alternately bob-bing up and then disappearing.

As the passengers emerged from the small ship's café, they rolled about the deck like pebbles.

I veered off on my own; I had lost sight of Marjorie and Harold.

Through the thrashing rain, I groped my way toward the bow. I saw a shallow open hold lying ahead. If I could reach it I could shelter in it, or so I thought.

But it was occupied. Three tall Greek priests, in their black attire and hats, lay prone on cots. I heard their wordless moans. Next to them, strapped to a board, was a huge dead fish.

I found a thick coil of rope and sheltered in its empty center, curled up with no thought, only bodily fear that each breath I took would be my last.

Ultimately I fell asleep. I was awakened sometime later by a sailor as we approached the wharf in Palma de Majorca. The sea had grown flat as slate and was the same color.

AFTER HAROLD LEFT THE NEXT DAY FOR PARIS, MARJORIE AND I found rooms in the Spanish equivalent of an American board-inghouse just a few miles from Palma.

The name of the village escapes me; it was a thumbprint on the land. Yet I can see its kitchen half a century later: strings of onions and garlic hanging from big hooks screwed into the dark high wooden ceiling, an eggplant on the edge of a scarred round table, a large pot on a wood-burning stove, a fisherman entering, carrying a pailful of his fresh catch of squid.

I longed to see the villa where Chopin and George Sand had lived, and I discovered a long sandy road that I imagined led to it. An English poet, Robert Graves, was living there then, but in those distant days I had no more interest in him than I had in the pink villa that had belonged to Natasha Rambova, said to have been the mistress of Rudolph Valentino, and which Marjorie and I glimpsed on a long slope among other villas.

My month in Spain was ending in a few days. Marjorie had enough material for a full article on the political life in Spain at the time.

We were the closest of friends, ever since we had met in San Francisco several years earlier, yet though she offered to loan me money to prolong my stay on the island, I was reluctant to take it.

We spent two more days on Majorca, idling on the local beach in the sunlight. On one of those days, we went out in his boat with the fisherman, watching his spinners sink into the blue-eyed water of the bay.

On the next afternoon, our last, we followed a couple for a while after we'd overheard them speaking German. He was reading an old copy of *Fortune* magazine as he walked, his shoes sinking into the sand. Both were thin and tall; she was looking—disapprovingly, Marjorie and I told each other—out to sea.

On that same day, I found a long column of ants marching in the sand in the shade of some trees near the beach. I placed a large twig at the head of the column. The leader's feelers encountered the twig; it made a right angle and led the column in another direction. "Nature is crazy," Marjorie remarked.

We boarded a small ship that would take us to Barcelona; from there we would take a bus to a village at the foot of the Pyrenees.

We were sated with sights; a Gothic church, a thirteenth-century church, a Moorish palace we had visited in Palma, and sunshine and wine where we had stayed. It had all nearly done us in, by giving us the illusion that other lives might be possible.

Why not stay forever on that beach? But then we recalled a young woman and her infant on the streets of Palma, a black transparent shawl covering both of them; she was holding out the hand that was not holding the infant, begging. That was a more likely alternative in our dream of a different life.

WE ARRIVED AT A BORDER VILLAGE IN THE FOOTHILLS OF THE Pyrenees in the early afternoon. Marjorie had enough pesetas left to take a car to the Spanish-French border, but the single one in the village had been commandeered by four or five Englishmen. They offered us a crowded ride in the relic that passed for a taxi, laughing and joking inanely—British jokers, I thought then—but we ended up walking or, rather, climbing, up the mountains, led by a soldier from the local army post. He was a grim-faced sixteen-year-old, wearing a Himmler coat whose length impeded his stride. German fashions were still the rage in Spain in those days.

Mostly we saw his back as he led us up a narrow goat path

that curved and hairpinned its way ever higher. It was hard going, though the three of us were young and strong, and two of us were full of urgent purpose.

We rounded a moss-covered boulder. Fifty yards or so above us, alongside the ancient taxi driver who stood counting the pesetas they had paid him, were the Englishmen, standing on a bluff, cheering us on, and holding out bars of chocolate. "Jolly good show!" I heard one of them say as we came closer.

The border was marked by a thin metal cable looped across a narrow road. There were two French taxis waiting on the cable's other side; the Englishmen, waving to us, folded themselves into one and Marjorie and I took the other.

At the shed that housed Customs we took leave of each other, she to spend a week in the south of France, and me to go back to Paris. A bus facing east and a train facing north were both standing a few yards from the shed.

Marjorie went through easily and waved to me from the bus before there was a great grinding of gears and she was gone. Then it was my turn to enter the shed.

A stout woman in a uniform asked me to undress to my underwear. Her face had no discernible expression, but she behaved with bureaucratic indifference, a kind of impersonal brutality. She searched me and then pointed at another door in the shed. I dressed and stepped out of it, into France.

I SPENT ONE NIGHT IN A CHEAP HOTEL IN PARIS. THE INNER courtyard was glass-covered, and when I looked out a window at it, I saw that it was littered with used condoms. The next morning I boarded a train for Calais, where an American freighter was docked. It carried seven or eight passengers. I was one of them.

WHEN I SAW THE SHORELINE OF EUROPE RECEDING, WHEN IT became a blur and then nothing but the sea, I cried out. I was standing at the rail, aft, straining to hold on to one piece of the European world. What did I want? To undo my earlier life in America? I was afraid of the past, afraid of the future.

I could have stayed; I had been offered jobs in France and England and Warsaw. Why hadn't I taken one of them? There was something in me that resisted being an ex-patriot. Perhaps, as my father once observed, I am always driven back to places I have been before.

A fierce storm at sea, when we were in what one of the ship's officers called the "roaring forties," delayed us for three days. We hove to; the cook, unable to provide the passengers with regular meals, so bad was the ship's rolling, handed us sandwiches and glasses of water when he could. Another officer tied a lounger on deck for me when the wind had nearly died down. I was doused with salt water by waves breaking over the bow, a welcome distraction from my endless thoughts about the future. In my dream, I was barely a walk-on in my own life. I could only conceive of events over which I had no control.

A German woman, large, lumpy-fleshed, young, told me how she had been raped by Russian soldiers when they occupied Berlin just after the end of the war. She spoke breathlessly in heavily accented English. Her eyes flickered away from mine. I had the conviction that she had practiced those stories as she sat on the edge of her berth and that the Russians had not touched her.

When we docked in New York Harbor, I needed the assistance of a ship's officer to walk down the gangplank. I was barely able to take a step. Europe had been for me a liberation. I didn't want to leave the ship.

I recall a story my husband, Martin, told me. He had been a soldier in the Second World War. When he landed on Omaha Beach—it wasn't long after D-Day and the horrors of war lay all about, in the water and on the beach; rain was falling; the soldiers labored up the muddy embankment between signs reading MINES! in different languages—he exclaimed, "I'm in Europe!"

I HAD A FEW JOB INTERVIEWS IN NEW YORK CITY AND TOOK one with a public relations firm. And I found a small West Side apartment with a kitchenette and a bedroom. But I was not able to forget the question a taxi driver had asked about me when I first disembarked from the freighter.

I had a few dollars left, so I could take a taxi that was parked on the wharf. As we drove to the window of the baggage department a few yards away, I heard the driver ask the clerk in a suspicious, hostile voice, after I had gotten out of the cab and picked up my suitcase, "Does she speak English?"

"Indeed I do," I said indignantly. It was the first time in my life in the United States that I had spoken out so boldly.

ASTRONOMY LESSON

One early evening I borrowed a station wagon from a social worker at Sleepy Hollow, an institution in Dobbs Ferry, New York. Seven adolescent boys hurled themselves into the seats, yelling, shouting, hitting, laughing. When I got in the driver's seat, they all calmed down somewhat. It was in the mid-1950s.

I had gotten the job as tutor through a friend. Sleepy Hollow was partly administered by the Manhattan School Authority; it was nondenominational. Most of the children were troubled and lived in cottages with an adult married couple. During the day they saw social workers. Some of them went out to the local public schools; half did not. They were defined as too antisocial by the psychiatrist who visited monthly.

They ranged in age from eleven to seventeen. They were

immensely excited that evening—getting away from the institution—and seemed to me to find even breathing a new sensation. They had all been brutalized when they were younger: incest, beatings, desertion, and—in one case, Jimmy's—left as an infant in a garbage dump. Another boy, the oldest, Frank, was black. He was tall and thin, quick on his feet, and, as he said about himself, made for basketball. But he didn't care for sports. What he was interested in was outer space. It was largely for him that I had made an arrangement with Dr. Lloyd Motz, the astronomy professor at Columbia University, to use their telescope on the roof of a building named Pupin. That was where we were headed that night.

Frank had spent most of his life in foster homes. He had a rootless quality; he always seemed on the point of departure. He perched on the edge of his desk and listened tolerantly while I tried to show him what a complete sentence was, but he was thinking of something else.

Someone had told me Frank was a sociopath, but I had difficulty attaching that word to him. He loved the talking part of my evenings at Sleepy Hollow, after the work was done in arithmetic or spelling or composition: the stories, the jokes we made, the tides of spoken memories.

I saw him angry only once. That was when the institution children, himself among them, went out to neighborhood schools, having been issued special food tickets because, it was said, they frequently spent the money they were allotted for lunch on cigarettes and candy. The local kids did too. Drugs were rarely available in those days.

Frank and the other children refused to go to school until the administration stopped the use of the food tickets. It was hard enough on them to be known as institution inmates, but to be so dramatically singled out as they were at the moment when they had to hand over their maroon tickets to the cafeteria cashier was intolerable to them. They were often bullied and baited by the local children, who exalted themselves and their own circumstances—whatever those might have really been— at the expense of the strangers in their midst, a form of cruelty not restricted to children.

When Frank was seven, he had asked his mother to take him to a movie. She said she couldn't; a friend was driving her to an appointment with a doctor. Frank told her he wished she was dead. She was killed in an automobile accident that afternoon, although the driver, her friend, was not seriously hurt. Frank's father had deserted his family several years earlier. There was no one to take care of Frank. He began his institutional life a few weeks after his mother had been killed.

I don't know how deeply, or in what part of his mind, he felt there was a fatal connection between his fleeting rage, the wish he had expressed that his mother die, and her death later that day. I know he suffered. His very abstraction was a form of suffering.

One night Frank lingered at the gatehouse where I held my classes. He asked me if I had ever been in another place like Sleepy Hollow. I said yes, once. Then for some reason I told him about the concentration-camp children I had met ten years earlier in the high Tatra Mountains in Poland. I spoke a little about the Holocaust. We were sitting on a step. It was a clear night in spring, with a little warmth in the air. The stars were thick.

"I never heard anything like that," he said. He asked me what had happened to those children in the mountains. I said I didn't know, except what happens to everyone—they would have their lives, they had endured and survived the horror of the camps, and each would make what he or she could of life. He looked up at the sky.

"What's after the stars?" he asked. "What's outside of all we're looking at?"

I named a few constellations I thought I recognized. Although his school grades were low, he'd read an astronomy textbook on his own. He corrected my star guesses twice. "But what do you think about way past out there?" he urged.

I said there seemed to be a wall in the mind beyond which one couldn't go on imagining infinity—at least, I couldn't. "Me neither," he said.

We sat for a few more minutes, then said good night and walked away from the gatehouse, me to my car and he to the cottage where he would live a few months longer before he ran away and was not heard from again.

The children in that residence accepted a certain amount of discipline—do your homework, eat the carrots before the cupcake—though they complained noisily. What they really hated was to be told how and what they were. They had heightened sensitivities to questions that were not questions but sprang from iron-clad assumptions about them and their troubles.

There were many people on the staff who were sure they knew everything. They had forgotten—if they had ever known—that answers are rarely synonymous with truth.

Those staff members were imprisoned in their notions as

much as the children they met with weekly were prisoners of case-history terminology. Each profession requires a system of reference and language to express it, but the cost to truth is high if there is no reflection of other possibilities beyond their systems of judgment.

"What's outside of all we're looking at?" Frank had asked.

Driving the station wagon to Columbia University that evening, I was hoping the telescope might show a thing or two.

I'd not been there myself. Dr. Motz had advised me that the atmosphere in New York City was so filthy we would be lucky if we glimpsed Venus. Columbia owned another viewing tele-scope in South Africa where, of course, astronomers had better visibility. As I parked on Broadway, the boys had begun to sing raucously, except for Frank, who told me later that he had been sweating with excitement.

I led my group to the Pupin building at the north end of the campus, where we took an elevator to the top. Duckboards cov-ered the tar roof and the gravel scattered over it. All around us were twinkling city lights, like stars. The wind was blowing so hard it was difficult to open the door. The boys whooped as they clustered around the entrance.

Inside was the assistant to Dr. Motz, who'd been told we were coming. An enormous slice of the sky—it was clear that night, as clear as it could be in New York City—was visible in the domed roof far above us. A curved metal section had been retracted, and the huge telescope was aimed through it at space. The assistant looked through the eyepiece on one side of the telescope and adjusted it for what seemed an hour; then he ges-tured to me to look. The boys were silent as they stood behind

me in the dimly lit room. On their own, they had formed a small line.

I looked and saw at once a rose-colored pulsating marshmallow—water vapor, the assistant explained—that was the planet Venus. Then I saw the rings of Saturn, tides of gases, a myriad of star clusters and, close up, the sweet moon, pitted with craters and reassuring in all that vastness. It was as though I had swung through space on a swing whose ropes extended from unimaginable depths of the darkness all around.

I stepped back and motioned the boys forward, one by one. Frank was last, and he spent the longest time looking through the eyepiece.

It took more than an hour. Then we went back over the duckboards and down the elevator. The boys didn't speak on the drive back to Sleepy Hollow. I heard someone sigh.

It took me a few days to understand their silence that night. I had imagined, at first, that it was because they had seen things that were larger than themselves, that gave them new perspectives on their lives, on everyone's life—the usual sentimental relativism.

But now I think they were quiet because for the first time, in the observatory at Columbia, they had seen something other than themselves.

I too had had that experience ten years earlier. The Second World War had caused devastation all over Europe, and millions upon millions of people had been slaughtered, yet my year over there had shown me something beyond my own life, freeing me from chains I hadn't known were holding me, showing me something other than myself.